The Second Coming
1998

The Second Coming 1998

Edgar Cayce's Earth-Change Prophecies

Kirk Nelson

A.R.E. Press • Virginia Beach • Virginia

A.R.E. Press
68th Street & Atlantic Avenue
P.O. Box 656
Virginia Beach, VA 23451-0656

Library of Congress Cataloging-in-Publication Data
 The second coming 1998 : Edgar Cayce's Earth change prophecies / Kirk Nelson
   p.   cm.
 ISBN 0-87604-406-2
 1. Cayce, Edgar, 1877-1945–Prophecies. 2.Second Advent. 3. Prophecies (Occultism)   I. Title.
 BF 1027.C3N45   1998
 133.3–dc21   97-49140
                                                                      CIP

Temple photo courtesy of the *Biblical Archaeology Review* (March -April 1983 issue), 300 Connecticut Avenue, Washington, D.C. 20008

Edgar Cayce readings © 1971, 1993, 1994, 1995, 1996
by the Edgar Cayce Foundation.
All rights reserved.

Cover design by John Comerford and Kim Cohen

To Sandra

Table of Contents

INTRODUCTION

America's greatest psychic, Edgar Cayce, said that 1998 would be the most significant year of change in the history of humanity. Dramatic earth changes, exploding spiritual awareness, the return of Jesus, and the beginning of a golden age of peace on earth were all predicted by Cayce for the year 1998. These exciting predictions are what this book is all about.

Cayce is not the only source of prophetic information we will examine, however. We will look at prophecies from the Bible, the Dead Sea Scrolls, the Hopi Indians, Nostradamus, and astrology.

After we find out what is prophesied, the timetable of events, and when these events are likely to occur, we will learn what we, individually and collectively, can do to prepare ourselves for them.

Lest we take any predictions too seriously, we should remember the case of William Miller, whose story is retold in the following quote from the book, *Did Jesus Write This Book?* by Charles Francis Potter:

"The nineteenth and twentieth centuries have also produced prophecies of the 'end of days.' The last century brought the once famed William Miller, an American who founded a sect named after himself. Like his predecessors of the A.D. 999 hoax, Miller calculated his end-all date from biblical mathematics, particularly those obscure calculations in Daniel (8:14). Christ will return on March 21, 1843, or March 21, 1844, Miller told his followers, who prepared their ascension robes in readiness for their translation into heaven. Twice the faithful gathered for the glorious meeting, and twice nothing happened. 'The World is reeling to and fro like a drunkard,' the leader assured the Millerites, but all that appeared in the sky were ominous rings around the sun, and the awesome tail of the great comet of 1843, measuring 108,000,000 miles in length.

"Sorrowfully, after this double fiasco, the only world to end was Miller's. Thousands of followers deserted him. A broken man, he died alone in his Vermont home, discredited and beaten by his own honest delusion."

Unlike the Millerites, we should not don our ascension robes and prepare for the end. But there are certain signs that will tell us when these great changes are close. These signs are, I believe, clearly discernible and will become apparent to all of us as the time draws near.

THE TEMPLE MOUNT

One of the great things about prophecy is that in chapter 24 of the Gospel of Matthew in the Bible, Jesus tells us all the things that will happen before He returns. For this reason it is the most important passage in the Bible with respect to prophecy. It begins as follows:

Matthew 24:3-22

And as he sat on Mount Olives, the disciples came to him privately saying, Tell us, when shall these things be? And what shall be the sign of your coming and the end of the age?

And Jesus answered them and said to them, Take heed that no man deceive you.

For many shall come in my name, saying, I am Christ; and shall deceive many.

And you shall hear of wars and rumors of wars; see that you are not troubled for all these things must come to pass, but the end is not yet.

For nation shall rise against nation, and kingdom

against kingdom; and there shall be famines, and pestilences, and earthquakes, in various places.

All these things are the beginning of sorrows.

Then shall they deliver you up to be afflicted and shall kill you; and you shall be hated of all nations for my name's sake.

And then shall many be offended and shall betray one another.

And many false prophets shall rise and shall deceive many.

And because iniquity shall abound, the love of many shall grow cold.

But he that shall endure to the end, the same shall be saved.

And this gospel of the kingdom shall be preached in all the world for a witness to all nations; and then shall the end come.

When you, therefore, shall see the abomination of desolation, spoken of by Daniel the prophet, stand in the holy place (whoever reads let him understand).

Then let them who are in Judea flee into the mountains;

Let him who is on the housetop not come down to take anything out of his house;

Neither let him who is in the field return back to take his clothes.

And woe to those who are with child, and to those who nurse children in those days!

But pray that your flight be not in the winter, neither on the sabbath day;

For then shall be great tribulation, such as was not since the beginning of the world to this time, no, nor ever shall be.

And except those days should be shortened, there should no flesh be saved; but for the elect's sake those days shall be shortened.

The Abomination of Desolation

What is an abomination of desolation? It is a term that refers to the desecration of the Jewish temple in Jerusalem. This desecration occurs when a sinful object is brought into the sacred part of the temple, where only the priests are allowed to enter. An example would be if a pig were offered on the holy altar, or if an altar to a pagan god were built in the holy place. A Syrian king, Antiochus Epiphanes, defiled the temple in just such a manner in 165 B.C. In order for another abomination of desolation to occur, the Jews must build a new temple.

The last Jewish temple in Jerusalem was destroyed in 70 A.D. by the invading Romans. However, since the Israelis recaptured Jerusalem in the 1967 war, they have begun excavating the ancient temple site. This has created a problem because the Moslem holy place, the Dome of the Rock, is built on the site of the old Jewish temple. This makes the Temple Mount sacred to both the Moslems and the Jews, and both claim it as their own. We can see how important the temple site is to the Jews from this description of the Israelis' capture of the Temple Mount in 1967 after 2,000 years of dispersement:

"The Israeli paratroop commander Mordechae Gur from atop Mount Olives ordered the final assault on the temple mount, 'For two thousand years our people have prayed for this moment. Let us go forward.'

"Colonel Gur could not wait. He raced his halftrack down the mountain at top speed, hurling

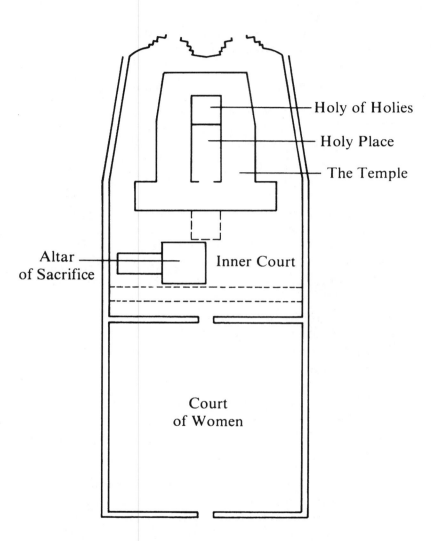

Diagram of the ancient Jewish Temple

past the burned-out hulks of tanks and the sprawling bodies of slain paratroopers, then dodged by a flaming truck partly blocking St. Stephen's Gate and burst right into the Old City. White flags were beginning to appear on all sides. While his paratroopers reared in behind him, the colonel turned left, crashed through another gate and then sent back his message to GHQ: 'The Temple Mount is ours. Repeat: The Temple Mount is ours.' And despite the crackle of continued sniper fire, the first paratroopers rushed to the Western Wall, touched and kissed the sacred stones, then burst into tears at their triumph."*

The Western Wall is a holy place to the Jews because it is the outside wall of the temple that was destroyed in 70 A.D. Recently they have begun to excavate the area near it and the steps that led to the temple on the other side of the mount along the Southern Wall. Over the years layer after layer of debris has built up on the site of the old temple, and it will take some time to uncover it.

In the Book of Exodus in the Old Testament are instructions for the construction of the temple and also instructions on how to perform the temple worship. Part of this worship involves the sacrificing of animals. This sacrifice is so important to the Jews that when they recaptured the Temple Mount in 1967, they wanted to begin again this daily ritual. The reason they did not is that they did not know the location of the old altar, since it is buried beneath the site of the Dome of the Rock.

The exact location of the temple's altar is important because according to Jewish law the sacrifice can only take place on the exact spot of the original altar. For many years it has been theorized that the altar was located under the Moslem holy place, the Dome of the Rock, from where,

*Time magazine, April 12, 1982, p. 30, New York, N.Y., "City of Protest and Prayer," Otto Friedrich.

according to legend, Mohammed ascended into heaven.

Religious zealots in Israel have already begun a campaign to rebuild the temple. Geula Cohen, a member of the Israeli Parliament, plans to introduce legislation that would open the Temple Mount to Jewish worshipers. Groups such as the Faithful of the Temple Mount (based in Israel) and the Jewish Temple Foundation (based in Denver, Colorado) are also calling for the Third Temple to be built. This movement has gone so far in Israel that a Jewish college in Jerusalem has begun training students in the rites prescribed for the priests in the temple!

A few years ago Israel's chief archaeologist Yigael Yadin translated and published a 2,000-year-old sacred writing called the Temple Scroll. In this scroll is an exact description of the dimensions of the temple and the location of all the temple's inner furnishings. This could provide a blueprint for the rebuilding of the temple.

In recent years some archaeologists have come to believe that the Jewish temple was actually located farther north than the Dome of the Rock. There is a small dome covering exposed bedrock on the northern edge of the Temple Mount. It is known as the Dome of the Tablets and is now believed to be the spot where the inner sanctuary, the holy of holies, was located. If it proves to be *the* location of the holy of holies, then the temple could be rebuilt without disturbing the Moslem temple. This would remove a considerable obstacle to the building process, since disturbing the Dome of the Rock would cause a great outcry among the Moslems.

Jesus tells us that the abomination of desolation will "stand in the holy place." This is a very specific reference to part of the temple. The inner sanctuary of the temple has two parts: the holy place and the holy of holies. Only the priests in their daily ritual are allowed to enter the holy place. It is the spot where they burn incense and light the

Photo by Hershel Shanks

*In the foreground is the Dome of the Tablets where the holy of holies
was located. In the background is the Dome of the Rock.*

lampstand. The holy of holies is the most sacred part of the temple, which only the high priest is allowed to enter once a year on the Day of Atonement. On that day, the high priest enters the holy of holies and sprinkles the blood of the sacrifice to make atonement for the sins of the Jewish people. So the abomination of desolation will not take place in the innermost sanctuary but in the holy place just outside.

It is possible, however, that the abomination of desolation could occur without the temple being rebuilt. The term could refer to the desecration of the Temple Mount itself rather than a rebuilt temple.

For this reason events involving the Temple Mount should be watched closely in the future. Recently the Temple Mount was the focus of conflict when an Israeli soldier described as "mentally ill" stormed the Dome of the Rock Mosque and began shooting into a crowd of worshipers. Several people were killed before the attacker could be subdued. Israel's chief rabbinate denounced the attack, saying, "By this despicable act of opening fire on innocent people, the gunman desecrated the holiest site of the Jewish people and removed himself from the Nation of Israel."

After the attack on the Temple Mount, the Arab world reacted angrily. The king of Saudi Arabia called for a one-day strike throughout the region in protest. A Saudi newspaper called for a jihad or holy war to liberate Islam's holy site from Israeli occupation. On the Israeli-occupied West Bank of the Jordan River, Palestinian mobs rioted and stoned cars. In New York the Jewish Defense League condemned the attack, but called the attacker "a hero who tried to liberate the Temple Mount from the hands of foreigners." As these examples show, both sides view the Temple Mount as their sacred land and react violently to any disturbance of it.

Who Will Desecrate the Temple Mount?

The desecrator of the temple is referred to as the Anti-Christ by fundamentalist Christian prophecy writers. I think the term "desecrator" is more descriptive and more accurate, but "Anti-Christ" is the term most people are familiar with. Who this Anti-Christ might be, we can't say for certain, but we will examine several possibilities in the next chapter.

The Great Tribulation

After the abomination of desolation Jesus tells us that there will be a great tribulation, a time of trouble more tumultuous than any time that ever has been or will be on the earth. The events in this time period may involve war in the Middle East and earth changes.

There will not be a full-scale nuclear war, however. In Matthew 24 Jesus says that if this time were not cut short, then no one would be saved. So, clearly, any conflicts during this time will end before they lead to all-out nuclear war. Jesus' reference to total destruction shows that Jesus foresaw the invention of nuclear weapons and the ultimate question that we are now faced with, "Do we live in peace or do we destroy ourselves?"

Daniel's Final Seven-Year Period

In chapter 9 of the Book of Daniel, Daniel gives a series of prophecies. These involve many seven-year periods called "weeks" of years. Daniel's final seven-year period before the Second Coming is called Daniel's "seventieth week."

This final seven-year period begins with what Daniel calls the "confirmation of the covenant with many." The covenant referred to here is the covenant of the Jews with God that Palestine is to be their land. I interpreted this to mean that Daniel's final seven-year period would begin with many different countries confirming Israel's right to exist.

When I originally published this book in 1986, I predicted that Israel would receive diplomatic recognition from her enemies in 1991. In the fall of 1991, Israel sat down with her former enemies for the first time in history at the Madrid Peace Conference. I believe this fulfilled Daniel's prophecy.

Imagine how stunned I was to see Bible prophecy being fulfilled on my television screen. Even though I had predicted the timing, it still seemed amazing to me. I have no doubt we will see more prophecy being fulfilled in the near future.

The Invasion of Israel

Edgar Cayce was the greatest psychic in American history. He lived from 1877-1945 and gave over 14,000 readings, the majority of which were recorded and are still preserved. Cayce's expertise was diagnosing illness, and most of his readings were devoted to healing the sick. Cayce would lie on his couch, go into trance, and after being given only the name and address of the sick person, would give an accurate diagnosis including the appropriate remedies. Cayce's abilities were so profound that his fame put him on the front page of the magazine section of the *New York Times* on October 9, 1910.

The followers of Edgar Cayce formed an organization called the Association for Research and Enlightenment, Inc., to study and research his psychic readings. The A.R.E., with headquarters in Virginia Beach, still exists today and boasts a membership of over 30,000. The headquarters contains a large library, bookstore, and records of Cayce's 14,000 readings.

Edgar Cayce gave approximately 2,000 life readings.

These involve reincarnation, personal and business problems, and sometimes prophecy. The readings in which Cayce gave prophetic information are the ones that are of interest to us.

In one of these readings Cayce accurately predicted a real estate boom for Virginia Beach, including the year in which it would end. Years before it happened, he stated in a reading that Norfolk would be the number one seaport on the east coast surpassing New York. This is now the case.

Another of Cayce's predictions was that the lost continent of Atlantis would be discovered off the coast of the Caribbean island of Bimini in 1968 or 1969. This prophecy was fulfilled by a group of divers who discovered large rectangular stones beneath the ocean just off Bimini's shore. Much of the later discoveries involving these stones are chronicled in Dr. David Zink's book, *Stones of Atlantis*. Dr. Zink mapped and explored the ruins and brought forth evidence that these rock formations were man-made. Amazing as it is, Cayce predicted the location and the year that the "stones of Atlantis" would be discovered.

Another prediction Cayce made was that a crystal power source would be discovered by scientists in 1958. The main theoretical papers that led to the invention of the laser (which uses a ruby crystal to amplify light) were put forward in 1958. Once again, Cayce was correct as to the year and the event.

The above-mentioned fulfilled prophecies show that Edgar Cayce had the ability to predict the future. This is not to say, however, that Cayce's predictive powers were infallible. He forecast earth changes for the state of Alabama in the 1930s that did not come about. The "sleeping prophet" always insisted that humans had free will and by acting in accordance with God's laws could change the future. Frequently, he stated that a group of people praying together could save a city, a state, or a region. This seems to be what happened when Cayce's predictions did not come true.

The Cayce readings contain several references which apply to our study of the Anti-Christ, and here is the first of these:

> **As is indicated in that period where entrance is shown to be in that land that was set apart, as that promised to that peculiar peoples, as were rejected – as is shown in that portion when there is the turning back from the raising up of Xerxes as the deliverer from an unknown tongue or land, and again is there seen that this occurs in the entrance of the Messiah in this period – 1998.** (5748-5)

The wording of this reading is a little awkward, but if examined closely it reveals its meaning. Cayce in the first part of this reading is speaking of the first entrance of Jesus to the earth "in that period," namely the first century A.D. The entrance point was Bethlehem, part of the promised land or, as Cayce puts it, "that promised to that peculiar peoples." The phrase "as were rejected" refers to the rejection of the Jews by God when they were carried into Babylonian captivity. The next phrase is the key point. Cayce states that there was a "turning back from the raising up of Xerxes as the deliverer" and that this would occur again during the entrance of the Messiah in the year 1998. The "Messiah" Cayce is referring to is Jesus, so this is one of the readings in which Cayce predicts that Jesus will return in 1998. This is easy to see, but the reference to Xerxes requires some historical background.

Xerxes was a very powerful Persian king who assembled an enormous army, conquered Greece, and burned Athens to the ground. His army is considered to be the largest army ever assembled in ancient times. Xerxes' rule stretched from Greece to India and included Arabia, the

Holy Land, Persia, and Egypt. He was described as "lecherous and cruel" and was well known as a desecrator of temples! Sounds very much like the Anti-Christ, doesn't it?

Wherever Xerxes went, he burned down and destroyed temples established to worship local deities. Preceding Persian kings had attempted to appease their subject people by respecting local gods, but Xerxes did just the opposite. He wrecked temples in Egypt, Babylon, and Greece. In Babylon, he went into the temple of Zeus, stole a gold statue of the ancient god, and killed a priest who attempted to stop him.

All of this would be enough to show us that Cayce was alluding to the Anti-Christ in this reading, but when you examine the relationship between the Persian kings and the Jews, the parallels become amazing. The four most important Persian kings mentioned in the Bible were:

Cyrus the Great (r. 550-530 B.C.) Darius (r. 521-486 B.C.) Xerxes (r. 486-465 B.C.) Artaxerxes (b. 465-425 B.C.)

Cyrus the Great conquered the Babylonians and permitted the Jews to return to the Holy Land and rebuild the temple. Artaxerxes, the son of Xerxes, allowed the Jewish leader Nehemiah to return to Jerusalem and rebuild the walls of the city. The story of this is in the biblical Books of Ezra and Nehemiah. As you can see, the Persian kings were deeply involved in the return of the Jews to the Holy Land, the reestablishment of the temple worship, and the rebuilding of the walls of Jerusalem. Considering that the Anti-Christ is expected to be instrumental in dealings to allow the Jews to keep Jerusalem and reestablish temple worship, the similarity between the Anti-Christ and the ancient Persian kings is striking.

But what about Xerxes? After Darius died, there was some debate as to who would be the new king. Xerxes was chosen because he was the oldest son of Darius and

because he had a kingly look and manner. The Book of
Esther in the Old Testament records the history of Xerxes
and the Jews. In the Old Testament Xerxes is known by his
Hebrew name, Ahasuerus. Cayce describes him in the
following paragraph:

> . . .Ahasuerus [Xerxes] came to the throne in the
> early twenties, and was not an uncouth man; yet –
> with the ease of the conditions and surroundings –
> being lauded by the princes of the various charges
> over which the counselors came – he became
> rather what would be termed in the present as a
> dissipated man. He was one, though, fair in the
> GENERAL outlook but with a very decided Roman
> nose (as would be called in the present), with hazel
> eyes, with fair hair; the weight being a hundred and
> seventy-six pounds (as would be termed in the
> present: then called duets [?]). This was his general
> mien.   (1096-3)

Xerxes was a tall, kingly looking man when he assumed
the throne, but because of the ease of conditions he
gradually eroded into what Cayce called a "dissipated
man." It would seem that this was his condition at the time
the Book of Esther was written, for the first part of Esther
describes Xerxes as feasting and drinking for seven days in
his palace. During this drinking bout he ordered his
beautiful queen, Vashti, to come and dance for the
entertainment of his guests, but she refused. This made
Xerxes decide to dethrone her and choose a new queen.
He felt that Vashti's refusal would cause women
throughout his kingdom to refuse the commands of their
husbands.

So the search went out for a new queen, one of great
beauty to be chosen. Ultimately, Esther, a Jew, was chosen.
However, Xerxes did not know that she was a Jew, because
she had been told by Mordecai, her kinsman, not to reveal

this to the king. During Esther's reign as queen, Haman, one of the king's advisors, convinced the king that the Jews were an evil people and that they should be destroyed. Xerxes issued the following proclamation:

Esther 3:13

And the letters were sent by posts into all the King's provinces, to destroy, to kill, and cause to perish, all Jews, both young and old, little children and women, in one day even upon the thirteenth day of the twelfth month, which is the month Adar, and to take the property of them for spoil.

So after being friendly with the Jews and letting them work on the rebuilding of the temple begun under Cyrus, Xerxes changed his mind and ordered all the Jews in his kingdom killed. This is exactly the scenario that interpreters of Bible prophecy have predicted for the end times: a powerful leader will make a deal with the Jews, allow them to reestablish temple worship, and then turn against them.

As students of the Bible know, Xerxes' mind was eventually changed by his Queen Esther, and he did not kill all the Jews. But Cayce was drawing a parallel here of a leader who was a friend to the Jews at first and later changed his mind. One thing to remember is that Cayce was an avid student of the Bible, having read it cover to cover once for every year of his life. Therefore, he was familiar with the story of Xerxes in the Book of Esther and with the fact that a future "Xerxes" was prophesied in the Bible.

The Invader

On September 25, 1939 (twenty-four days after the beginning of World War II), Edgar Cayce was asked the following question:

Q. For what real purpose is the present war?

A. Read in Daniel, the last two chapters, and see; also the 31st of Deuteronomy – and we will see. (257-211)

This reading was given for a Jewish man who wanted to know the real purpose of World War II. Cayce repeatedly stated in other readings that the reason for Hitler's rise to power in Germany was so that the Jews would return to their own land, Palestine. Chapter 31 of Deuteronomy, which Cayce recommended to this man, has to do with the return of the Jews to their own land. In this chapter of Deuteronomy Moses lectures the Jews just before they are to cross the Jordan River into Palestine.

What Cayce is saying in the above reading is that World War II was the catalyst for the Jews' return to their own land and the fulfillment of the prophecies of the last two chapters of Daniel. At the end of World War II, part of the settlement agreement stated that because of the extermination camps and the persecution of the Jews by the Germans, the Jews needed a homeland. Palestine was selected and ultimately given up by the British to provide a homeland for the Jews.

The last two chapters in Daniel are Daniel 11 and 12. These chapters predict an invasion of the Middle East prior to the Second Coming. The parts of these chapters that concern us are the last verses of Daniel 11 and all of Daniel 12:

Daniel 11:40-45

And at the time of the end shall the King of the South push at him; and the King of the North shall come against him like a whirlwind, with chariots, and with horsemen, and with many ships; and he shall enter into the countries, and shall overflow and pass through.

He shall enter also into the glorious land, and

many countries shall be overthrown, but these shall escape out of his hand, even Edom, and Moab, and the chief of the Children of Ammon.

He shall stretch forth his hand also upon the countries, and the land of Egypt shall not escape.

But he shall have power over the treasures of gold and of silver, and over all the precious things of Egypt; and the Libyans and the Ethiopians shall be at his steps.

But tidings out of the east and out of the north shall trouble him; therefore, he shall go forth with great fury to destroy, and utterly to sweep away many.

And he shall plant the tabernacles of his palace between the seas in the glorious holy mountain; yet he shall come to his end, and none shall help him.

Daniel 12:1

And at that time shall Michael stand up, the great prince who stands for the children of your people and there shall be a time of trouble, such as never was since there was a nation even to that same time; and at that time your people shall be delivered, every one that shall be found written in the book.

This passage deals with an invasion of the Middle East by a future king. He will enter the glorious land (Israel) and pass through into Egypt. We know that these verses refer to the time of the end because the passage begins with the phrase "at the time of the end." Plus, the events described in this section of Daniel have never been fulfilled.

This next point is very, very important. Verse 1 of Daniel 12 shows us that the invasion will occur at the beginning of the tribulation because the wording of this verse is identical to Jesus' description of the tribulation in Matthew 24. Jesus was familiar with the book of Daniel and realized that He was quoting from Daniel in describing the events preceding His return. He and Daniel both say that the tribulation will be a time of trouble such as never seen before. Verse 11:45 states that the invader will "plant the tabernacles of his palace between the seas in the glorious holy mountain." It is possible that the mountain referred to is not only the land of Israel but the Temple Mount itself in Jerusalem. So after the invasion the invader will set up his headquarters in Israel, possibly in Jerusalem.

The military aspects of this war in the Middle East provide us with clues as to who the invader will be. Daniel says that the Libyans and the Ethiopians "shall be at his steps." This means they will be servants of the invader or, as it is called in war, allies. This is not surprising, since both Libya and Ethiopia are at present bitter enemies of Israel.

Daniel states that the lands of Edom and Moab and Ammon will escape invasion. These names were used in biblical times to describe what is now the country of Jordan.

This fits, since Jordan is a traditional enemy of Israel.

One of the most interesting aspects in all this is that both Israel and Egypt will be invaded and possibly allied together against the invader. Until the Camp David agreement of a few years ago, establishing peace between Egypt and Israel, this would not have seemed possible. Now this would seem to be more than likely.

After Egypt and Israel are subdued, the invading king will be disturbed by tidings out of the North and East and shall go forth to kill many people. But as Daniel tells us, he will come to his end, and no one will help him. Whether he will be destroyed by men or by an act of God is not made clear, but he will ultimately be destroyed.

The Michael written of in Daniel 12 is Michael the Archangel. He is the Lord of the Way. He will deliver the souls of all that are written in the Book of Life. Those who have followed the true spirit of the Christ Consciousness, whatever their religion, will be delivered.

Before this, however, a great military power must arise and defeat Israel and Egypt in a war, and this will take a very strong army indeed.

There is considerable debate over whether the Anti-Christ and the invader will be the same person or whether the invader will be attacking the Anti-Christ. If the invader is separate from the Anti-Christ, the "Xerxes" Cayce referred to might be the invader, not the Anti-Christ. He would be seen as a "deliverer" rescuing the Israelis from the Anti-Christ, but in fact the Israelis would be trading one oppressor for another.

Whether the invader and the Anti-Christ are the same person or not, there are four places from which they or he might come.

The Common Market

One of the most popular of several theories about the Anti-Christ is that he will be the head of the European Economic Community or, as it is known, the Common Market. The main reason for popularity of this theory is that the European Economic Community (EEC) covers the area of the ancient Roman Empire as predicted in Daniel.

Another reason for the popularity of this theory is that the Common Market became a ten-nation group on January 1, 1981. Many scholars of Bible prophecy believe that the Anti-Christ will be the head of a ten-nation group.

The EEC has since picked up several other members but still bears close examination. Europe holds a pivotal position in world affairs, and united into one force it would have remarkable economic and political strength. The main reason the EEC was formed was to create a unified European economic power to compete with the United States and Japan. This is important because economic control is theorized to be the way in which the Anti-Christ will gain power over the world. Revelation tells us that no man will be able to buy or sell without the number of the beast on his hand or his forehead, and the number of the beast is 666. One suggested meaning for this is that 666 represents a credit number which, much like a credit card number, each person will have to use when he or she makes a purchase or a monetary transaction. This number could be tattooed on the hand, invisible except when read by a special machine. Such a system could be introduced as an alternative to the use of cash. With a computerized credit system a government leader could control all transactions within an economy, and this may be the way the Anti-Christ obtains world power.

A new economic order will have to be set up if the world economy crashes as it did in the 1930s. Over the last two decades, Third World countries have built up an enormous debt to the industrialized nations. If this debt is not paid, it could bring about just such an economic collapse. The EEC would be central to any economic reorganization, since it is a trading partner both to the West and to the East.

Militarily, Europe has become more involved in the Middle East and Africa in recent years. European troops were moved into Beirut in 1982 as part of the multinational peacekeeping force. France sent its troops and planes to Chad in North Africa in 1983 to halt a Libyan invasion of that country. European forces also participated in the attack on Iraq during the recent Persian Gulf War. These types of military or political involvements in the Middle East by the Europeans should be watched closely in the coming years, especially any with Israel.

Any incidents of anti-Semitism in Europe should also be watched carefully. In the 1980s there were a number of terrorist attacks on Jews in Europe, including a shooting spree at a Jewish restaurant in Paris. Also in Paris, the

Israeli airline El Al had one of its ticket counters bombed in an attack that injured seven people. In what many considered the most frightening incident, Italian strike demonstrators shouted, "Jews to the ovens!" as they marched past a synagogue in Rome. These events show that the hatred of the Jews fomented by the Nazis in Europe many years ago is still in existence today.

When the theory of a European Anti-Christ was first popularized, no one could have imagined the changes that would occur with the collapse of communism in Eastern Europe. This would seem to make the possibility of a European Anti-Christ less likely, although there are still extremist political groups in Europe fostering hatred and bigotry. Whether they could gain control of the whole EEC remains to be seen.

The Arabs

The worst enemies the Jews have in the world today are the Arabs. For the forty years of Israel's existence, the Arabs have repeatedly fought wars in a vain attempt to destroy Israel. Arab leaders have called for a jihad or "holy war" against Israel in order to liberate the Moslem holy places in Jerusalem. The reason for this feeling is that Israel was formed out of Palestine, an area in which the Arabs have lived for thousands of years.

Recently Israel and her Arab enemies sat down at the conference table for the first time ever at the 1991 Middle East Peace Conference. Does this mean that Israel and her enemies are finally going to make peace? I don't think so. Israel joined the conference under enormous pressure from the United States. The Arab states joined in hopes of regaining land that they lost in the 1967 Arab-Israeli war. A diplomatic agreement may come out of the conference, but I don't think it will be a permanent peace.

One thing to watch for in the peace conference is any

sort of deal involving the Temple Mount. As mentioned before, according to Jewish law the Jewish temple has to be built in Jerusalem on the same site where it was built 2,000 years ago. Right now the Moslem holy place, the Dome of the Rock, is located on that site. To rebuild the temple, the Israelis may have to make some kind of agreement with the Moslems. This agreement may come out of the peace talks.

Cayce spoke of the "raising up of Xerxes" as a precedent to the Second Coming. And who was Xerxes but a Persian king? Therefore Cayce may have been referring to a king from that region. Xerxes ruled from an area that is now on the Iran-Iraq border, and it's possible that the Anti-Christ will come from one of the countries in that area. He might enter into an agreement with the Israelis involving the Temple Mount or Israel's right to exist. The scene would be very much like the one when Egypt's president Anwar Sadat went to Jerusalem to make peace with the Israelis. The Anti-Christ would be seen as a great friend like Sadat, but unlike Sadat he would later reverse himself.

Also, Daniel and Revelation say that the kingdom of the desecrator will have control over the entire world. The Arab oil kingdoms through their oil have that kind of power. The oil sheiks could wreck the American economy by cutting off our oil supply. They could also devastate the economies of Japan, Europe, and the rest of the world. Saudi Arabia, for example, makes 120 billion dollars a year on oil sales. At that rate in ten years they could buy every share of stock on the New York Stock Exchange. In ten years this cash flow amounts to one trillion dollars, a staggering figure.

Another fact that would implicate the oil sheiks as a possible Anti-Christ is that their lifestyle is very much like that of Xerxes. They maintain harems, just like Xerxes did, and have a life of incredible wealth. Their kings are chosen by family relationships; usually the oldest male in the family succeeds. As we have seen, this is how the Persians chose their kings.

An Arab confederacy like the ten-nation group mentioned in the biblical prophecies is also possible. The Arabs have organizations like OPEC (Organization of Petroleum Exporting Countries) and the Arab League. With the amount of weapons they are buying from the United States and others and their combined economic clout, they could be a powerful force. Anyone who doubts this should look at the following list of the countries and populations and imagine them united under one leader:

Syria 8,000,000	South Yemen 2,000,000
Iraq 17,000,000	Kuwait 1,000,000
Iran 34,000,000	Yemen 6,000,000
Saudi Arabia 9,000,000	United Arab Emirates 255,000
Jordan 2,500,000	Oman 8,000,000

The total population of these countries is nearly 80 million, much larger than the population of Israel, which stands at five million.

Iran, the country on this list with the largest population, is one of the most radical of the Arab regimes. The fall of the shah created a vacuum of power that was filled by the Shiite Moslem leader, Ayatollah Khomeini. Khomeini claimed to be a religious leader but was actually a political one. His reign was the type of fusion of church and state that many have envisioned for the Anti-Christ. Khomeini was not the Anti-Christ, but his rule provides us with a good example of what an Arab Anti-Christ might be like.

Khomeini's regime was ruthless, to say the least. Executions of "dissidents" were carried out on a daily basis with little cause or pretext except guilt by association. The Revolutionary Guard, Khomeini's elite, terrorized opposing political factions with regularity. The people of the United States experienced their methods when they seized the American Embassy in Tehran in 1979. Fifty-two Americans were held against their will by these fanatics. Only the intervention of the Ayatollah himself prevented the execution of the American hostages.

Iran has called for radical revolutions in neighboring Arab countries to overthrow more moderate governments. This is a frightening development for a number of reasons. The assassina-tion of Egypt's president Sadat by Moslem fundamentalists demonstrated that anti-West feelings run deep in the Arab countries and that these feelings can change the political situation.

If these countries were to come under Moslem fundamentalist control, it could create a new Persian Empire complete with a new Xerxes. Along these lines, the Syrian government recently had to use its army to put down a Moslem rebellion that claimed many lives. Moslem fundamentalists took over the mosque in Mecca for several days in 1980 before Saudi police forces could capture them.

With a growing educated middle class in Saudi Arabia, the Saudi family will be hard pressed to maintain power. The pro-West Saudi royal family is one of the few ruling monarchies left in the world, and the fear is that a revolution could take place and topple them.

A Saudi Arabian Anti-Christ would be in a powerful position because of Saudi Arabia's wealth. They are using this wealth to increase the sophistication of their military by buying America's top fighter plane, the F-16, and the early warning radar plane, the AWACs. The sale of the AWACs to the Saudis caused quite a stir in the United States among people who felt the plane was too secret to be given to Saudi Arabia. The United Stated lost a lot of equipment when the shah of Iran was overthrown, and many people did not want to see the same mistake made again with the AWACs.

More and more, the Saudis have taken the important role of negotiator among the United States, Israel, and the more radical Arabs, such as the Palestine Liberation Organization and the Syrians. In recent years the Saudis again and again have been the go-between in cease fires between warring Israeli and Arab factions.

Another factor in this is the position of the Saudis as the official defenders of the Moslem holy places. As such, the Saudis would be involved in any negotiations concerning the Temple Mount and the Dome of the Rock. Years ago, the Israeli foreign minister Moshe Dayan tried to negotiate a treaty with the Saudis whereby the Israelis would keep Jerusalem, but Moslem flags would fly over Moslem holy places. This would have allowed the Moslems to have sovereignty over the holy places. This was rejected by the Saudis, but it shows how important their position is as the keeper of the Moslem holy sites.

As mentioned earlier, the style of the Saudi kings is similar to that of Xerxes. They are rich, powerful, and to some extent have absolute rule within their kingdom. Xerxes was chosen king because he was the oldest male, and this is the custom today in the Saudi royal family. He was also chosen because he had a kingly manner, another factor in the selection of a king among the Saudis. So, Cayce's reference to Xerxes could be a reference to a Saudi king.

When Saddam Hussein invaded Kuwait in 1990, many people in the United States wondered if he were the Anti-Christ. He saw himself as a latter-day Babylonian king, and he even claimed that the reason he invaded Kuwait was to liberate Jerusalem from the Jews. People were afraid that the Persian Gulf War would be the final conflict before the Second Coming of Jesus. Iraq had chemical, biological, and nuclear weapons programs that held out the possibility of war on a scale the world has never seen.

When Iraq began to fire Scud missiles into Israel, the

THE INVASION OF ISRAEL

Israelis armed their missiles with nuclear weapons and brought them out in the open so that the American spy satellites could see them. This put pressure on the Americans to get rid of the Scud missile sites in Iraq. This also showed that had Saddam used chemical weapons on Israel, Israel was prepared to respond with nuclear weapons if necessary.

The possibility of nuclear conflict in the Middle East grows with each passing year. Israel has by some estimates over 200 nuclear weapons. Iran and Algeria have been sold nuclear weapon technology by China, and there is no doubt they would use these weapons on Israel. Syria has been buying ballistic missiles, and Libya reportedly has offered millions of dollars to anyone who would sell them plutonium for a nuclear bomb. At the same time Saddam Hussein is still in power in Iraq and presumably still interested in furthering his nuclear weapons program.

It is easy to see from these examples how an Arab-Israeli war could easily turn into a nuclear war in the future as more and more countries obtain nuclear weapons. If the Arabs won, they could overrun Jerusalem and desecrate the Temple Mount. If this happens, it will be a case of history repeating itself. In 165 B.C. Antiochus Epiphanes, a Syrian king, desecrated the temple by sacrificing a pig on the altar and erecting a statue of a false god there. Antiochus is viewed as a type of past Anti-Christ and is probably a good model for the future one.

Russia

Russia has long been a persecutor of Jews both inside Russia and around the world. During the seventy-four years of communist rule in Russia, the enemies of Israel – whoever they might have been at the time – were invariably supplied by the Russians. This would include Egypt when they were at war with Israel and later the

Syrians. In almost every Arab-Israeli conflict, it was Russian weapons that killed Israelis on the battlefield.

But then the Berlin wall came down, and Eastern Europe was set free, and communism fell in Russia, and the Soviet Union divided up into the Commonwealth of Independent States. Does this mean the end of any threat from Russia?

Certainly, we are all happy to see the demise of the communist system in Russia, but we should temper our judgment with caution. There are certain aspects of this new revolution that need to be watched lest they give rise to a Russian Anti-Christ.

Former communists still occupy many of the government positions in Russia, and the president of Russia, Boris Yeltsin, is a former Politburo member. The Russian parliament is dominated by former communists, and they recently blocked reforms that were introduced by Yeltsin and his allies. Economic conditions are very tough in Russia right now, and the reform program that Yeltsin has put in place is not as popular as it was in the beginning. There have been huge price rises in basic commodities, and, as a result, some people have called for a return to the old system. We should not forget that the French Revolution which overthrew the monarchy was followed by the rise of Napoleon.

The mighty military machine the communists built is still intact, and this makes the situation dangerous. The army still has 50,000 tanks and 25,000 nuclear warheads, although the various republics have begun to fight over who gets to keep these. To defeat Israel, Egypt, and the other countries mentioned in Daniel 11 will require tremendous military power. It is a convincing argument that only one country in the world, Russia, could put that much power in the Middle East that quickly.

The reason for this can be seen very clearly by looking

at a map of the area. Russia is directly north of Israel, which means that the Russians have very easy access to Israel by land. American forces would have to arrive by air or sea, and outside of planes from U.S. carriers in the Mediterranean, the response would take too long. The United States is too far away from the area to act quickly, and this was seen in the Gulf War. It took the U.S. five months to build up enough troops to take on Iraq, which is a military midget compared to the Russians.

An invasion of Israel might provide the Russians with economic rewards. The invasion route between Russia and Israel includes Iraq's richest oil fields. This route includes Iran, Iraq, and Syria, three countries with no friendship treaties with the United States. The Russians might feel that the U.S. would do nothing to stop them in these countries and by the time they reached Israel, it would be too late.

It is also possible that all these countries might be united with Russia against Israel. Ezekiel 38 and 39 speak of an invasion of Israel by an army from the north that has been widely interpreted as the Russian army. Included in the invasion forces of Ezekiel 38 are troops from Persia (Iran), Put, and Cush (Libya and Ethiopia). Libya and Ethiopia were mentioned in Daniel 11 as being allied with the invader, so Ezekiel 38 and Daniel 11 may describe the same invasion. Certainly Iran, Libya, and Ethiopia would be anti-Israel in any case. Ezekiel predicts this invasion force will ultimately be destroyed by God in the form of fire.

The Soviet Union was made up of fifteen republics. When the Soviet Union broke up, the three Baltic republics left and became independent states. That left twelve republics who got together to form what is now called the Commonwealth of Independent States. The question that arises is this: Could the ten-nation group mentioned by Daniel come out of the former Soviet republics? The answer is, it may already have.

After the so-called coup in the Soviet Union in August
of 1991, the Soviet Union was organized into a ten-nation
group called the State Council. The head of this ten-
nation group was Mikhail Gorbachev.

In the 1986 edition of this book, I predicted that the
leader of a ten-nation group would confirm Israel's right to
exist with many nations in 1991, and that this would be the
beginning of Daniel's seven-year period. In October of
1991 Mikhail Gorbachev, the leader of a ten-nation group,
renewed diplomatic relations with Israel and opened the
1991 Middle East Peace Conference by calling on the
Arabs to recognize Israel's right to exist. These events fit
the prophecy perfectly. This, of course, would mean that
Gorbachev is the Anti-Christ. I realize how radical this
sounds, but the events of 1991 fit the prophecy amazingly
well. Because of this the career of Mikhail Gorbachev
bears a closer look.

Gorbachev's image around the world is that of a man
who single-handedly brought down the Iron Curtain and
established peace between East and West. But a closer
look shows a different reality than that of the slick media
image. Why did Gorbachev let Eastern Europe slide out
of the Soviet orbit? Was it out of the kindness of his heart,
or was it because the Soviet economy had crumbled so
completely that they could no longer afford to prop up
regimes in Europe? I believe that the Soviet system had
failed so badly that the communists had no choice but to
let Eastern Europe go in hopes of saving the Soviet Union.
And Gorbachev did a masterful job of putting the best face
on this collapse, making it look like an act of generosity
when it was, in fact, an act of desperation.

Gorbachev's rule inside the Soviet Union was far from
peaceful and could be quite ruthless when necessary.
When Soviet miners held a demonstration for indepen-
dence in the republic of Georgia, the protest was broken

up by army troops who hacked several of the miners to death with sharpened shovels. When an investigation of this brutality was called for, Gorbachev did nothing. No one was reprimanded; no one was tried for the crime. Gorbachev let it stand.

When the Baltic republics first tried to break away from the Soviet Union in the late 1980s, the KGB sent in special Black Beret troops to terrorize the population. In one demonstration protesters were run over by tanks and killed. In another case Black Beret troops shot and killed local border guards. Again Gorbachev did nothing.

The reason Gorbachev did nothing is that he wanted to save the communist system and stay in power at all costs. He said, "I am a communist, this may surprise you, but it should not." Gorbachev was the master at talking about reforms but not actually carrying them out. Former foreign minister Andrea Gromyko said this about Gorbachev: "This man has a nice smile, but with iron teeth."

There are some interesting parallels between the description of the Anti-Christ in Revelation and Daniel and the life of Mikhail Gorbachev. First, as mentioned, we are told that he will be the head of a ten-nation group. Then we are told that the ten leaders will have power for only a short time. Revelation 17:12 says the ten will hold power for only "one hour with the beast." The ten-nation State Council lasted only four months at the end of 1991.

We are also told that the Anti-Christ will have "a mouth speaking great things." Gorbachev's reputation for eloquence is well known. When he made a speech at the U.N., it was so impressive that people described it as being like one of President Kennedy's classic speeches.

Daniel 7:25 says the Anti-Christ will "think to change the times and the laws" and Revelation 13:7 says he will "have power over all kindreds, and tongues, and nations." Gorbachev made a speech in the U.S. in May of 1992 in

which he called for the creation of a one-world government
with economic, political, and military power – a government with the "teeth" to "punish" nations that misbehave.
We are told in Revelation 13:17 that people won't be
able to buy or sell without the "mark of the beast" on their
hands or in their forehead. Gorbachev has a prominent
birthmark on his forehead that people invariably bring up
when I mention him as a possible Anti-Christ. They think
this might be the mark of the beast. Edgar Cayce had this
to say about people with prominent birthmarks:

> **Take individuals everywhere, where there has
> been or is a mark in the body, and analyze their
> activity and associations among individuals; for
> their lives and their associations are different from
> the ordinary ken. Many will be found to have
> almost caused or averted tragedies (as called in the
> earth) in the lives of individuals.   (573-1)**

I realize that all this is speculation since Gorbachev at
the present time holds no public office and is out of power,
but this may also be part of the prophecy. Revelation 13
says that one of the beast's heads will be wounded as if to
death but that the deadly wound will be miraculously
healed. This may be a symbolic description of a leader who
is thrown out of power but later returns. During his 1992
visit to the U.S., Gorbachev implied that he planned a
return to power. He said, "DeGaulle returned to political
life at sixty-eight; I still have seven years left." Whether
this happens remains to be seen.

Whatever happens the remnants of the Soviet Union
need to be watched closely simply because of the enormous military power it contains. Any grouping of these
nations, whether led by Gorbachev or someone else, could
still be a threat.

China

Other than the EEC, the Arabs, and Russia, there is one other country that could be the invader or the Anti-Christ. That country is China.

Revelation 9:13-16

And the sixth angel sounded, and I heard a voice from the four horns of the golden altar which is before God,

Saying to the sixth angel who had the trumpet, Loose the four angels who are bound in the great river, Euphrates.

And the four angels were loosed, who were prepared for an hour, and a day, and a month, and a year, to slay the third part of men.

And the number of the army of the horsemen were two hundred thousand thousand; and I heard the number of them.

Revelation 16:12

And the sixth angel poured out his bowl upon the great river, Euphrates, and its water was dried up, that the way of the kings of the East might be prepared.

The preceding verses of the Bible have been interpreted as referring to an invasion of the Middle East by the Chinese. Revelation states that an army of 200 million will invade from beyond the Euphrates River, which is in what is now Iraq. Only one country in the world could put an army in the field of 200 million, and that is China. China has a militia of 200 million and a civilian population of over one billion people. China's geographic location is east of the Euphrates River from where we are told the kings of the East will come. In addition, we are told that it will be necessary to dry up the Euphrates River in order that this army might pass. There are dams in place on the

Euphrates that could shut off the river's flow. This is something that armies did in ancient times to provide easier passage, and Revelation says it will happen again.

Certain present-day events make this part of Revelation particularly disturbing. China turned more militant when thousands of peaceful demonstrators were shot down in Tiananmen Square in 1989. Any government willing to use its troops on its own people in such a ruthless manner certainly wouldn't hesitate to use them in foreign lands.

China is a nuclear power possessing over 1,000 nuclear weapons and has submarine-launched missiles that are invulnerable to attack. This is frightening when you consider that the Chinese could lose 100 million civilian casualties in a nuclear war and still have a billion people left. They are pre-paring for just such an eventuality by building one of the most extensive underground fallout shelter systems in the world under their capital city of Beijing. Underground tunnels run for miles, providing safety in case of nuclear war. The building of these tunnels shows that the Chinese consider nuclear war a strong possibility.

Because of the opening of relations with China, the United States has increased its trade commitment with the Chinese. These commitments include some materials with military applications such as heavy trucks and computers. This development prompted Russian novelist Aleksandr Solzhenitsyn to warn the United States not to arm China in hopes of neutralizing the Russians because if we armed China, we would be "giving away the other half of the world."

Anyone who believes that the Chinese have no interest in Middle Eastern politics should remember that PLO chief Yasser Arafat and Libyan strongman Colonel Quadafi were in China recently on friendly visits. China has repeatedly taken anti-Israeli positions in questions of foreign policy, and there is no reason to expect their position to change in the future.

The prospect of a Chinese invasion of the Middle East is frightening. To come overland from China would require an invasion of Afghanistan, Iran, Iraq, and Syria. This route, which includes the Khyber Pass in Afghanistan, has been used countless times in the past as an invasion route. The carnage from such an invasion would be the worst the world has ever seen. Nuclear weapons would be the only way to stop such a large army, and this would be an unacceptable option because of the civilian deaths it would cause in the countries being occupied. The Israelis would no doubt use their nuclear arsenal, which they call the "doomsday machine," but this would be puny against an army of untold millions. They would be like ants overrunning the landscape.

China's intention to invade the Middle East may have been revealed by recent actions. The Chinese have built a superhighway through the Himalayas to Pakistan. India protested this action to the United Nations as a threat to peace in Asia. The question is: Why would the Chinese build such a road unless to use it as an invasion route? Indeed for an army of 200 million to move such a long distance, an improved road system would be necessary. The Chinese have begun to put such a system in place.

There is also evidence in the following Cayce reading for a Chinese invasion:

If there is not the acceptance in America of the closer brotherhood of man, the love of the neighbor as self, civilization must wend its way westward – and again must Mongolia, must a hated people, be raised. (3976-15)

A concept that is constantly brought up in the Cayce readings is that the leadership of civilization is continuously moving westward. First came the Roman Empire, then the British Empire, and today we have the American "Empire,"

each farther west than the preceding. In the above reading
Cayce tells us that if the United States does not live up to
its obligations with respect to the love of its neighbors and
all humankind, then civilization will move west and the
Mongol hordes will again sweep the world. The modern-
day Mongol horde is, of course, China.

Since this reading says that a hated people of Mongolia
must again be raised, it would be good for us to look back
at the last time Mongolia was the center of an empire.

In the early thirteenth century, a Mongol tribal chieftain
named Temuchin began conquering a large area of
Mongolia. As his power grew, he organized a huge, swiftly
moving, well-disciplined army and assumed the name
Genghis Khan or "Very Mighty King." Genghis expanded
his empire to include China and large sections of Asia.
Khan's warriors were particularly noted for their savagery.
Genghis died in 1227, and his successors, Ogodei Khan and
Kublai Khan increased the size of the empire by further
conquest and made Beijing its capital city. By the late 13th
century, the Mongol Empire stretched from the Pacific
Ocean to the Black Sea and included the area of what is now
Afghanistan, Pakistan, Iran, Iraq, Central Russia, Hungary,
and Poland. The invasion route taken by the Mongols in
conquering these countries is the same one that China
would have to take to invade the Middle East today. All in
all, Cayce drew an excellent parallel for us.

The question is: Has the United States provided
enough leadership to prevent the Chinese from becoming
aggressive? It is doubtful, and this makes a Chinese
invasion a strong possibility and one we need to watch for.

The possible alignments in such a situation are
impossible to predict. It might be the Chinese and the
Russians against the United States and Israel. It might be
the United States and the Russians against the Chinese.
Neither the United States nor the Russians could use all

their weapons against the Chinese for fear of being exposed to the remaining superpower. A three-way superpower conflict is much more tricky than a two-way conflict. The result might be so terrible that, as Revelation says, a "third part of men" on the earth might be killed, as the Chinese would probably use germ warfare in addition to conventional and nuclear. A Chinese invasion would devastate the entire Middle East and much of Asia.

Summary

It is interesting to note what the Bible says about the cities involved in Middle East conflicts. The destruction of Sidon and Tyre in Lebanon is predicted in Ezekiel, and these two cities were devastated by the 1982 Israeli invasion. This prophecy has already been fulfilled. More important to the future conflict is the prediction in Isaiah that Damascus will be taken away from being a city, and will be made a ruinous heap. Damascus would be the central location of an Israeli-Syrian war and would be subject to destruction. It is also in line with the invasion route from Russia and China to Israel.

There are other possible areas of conflict. Daniel 11:44–45 says that "tidings out of the north and east will trouble" the invader and in the end "none shall help him." These seem to be references to battles in other locations outside of the Middle East.

EARTHQUAKES AND POLE SHIFTS

Both Edgar Cayce and the Bible tell us that during the end times there will be earth changes. Jesus tell us that these changes will occur after a period of tribulation:

Matthew 24:29-30

Immediately after the tribulation of those days shall the sun be darkened and the moon shall not give its light, and the stars shall fall from heaven, and the powers of the heavens shall be shaken.

And then shall appear the sign of the Son of man in heaven; and then shall all the tribes of the earth mourn, and they shall see the Son of man coming in the clouds of heaven with power and great glory.

Revelation 6:12-17

And I beheld, when he had opened the sixth seal and, lo, there was a great earthquake, and the sun became black as sackcloth of hair, and the moon became like blood;

And the stars of heaven fell to the earth, even as

a fig tree casts her untimely figs, when she is shaken of a mighty wind.

And the heaven departed as a scroll when it is rolled together; and every mountain and island were moved out of their places.

And the kings of the earth, and the great men, and the rich men, and the chief captains, and the mighty men and every slave, and every free man hid themselves in the dens and in the rocks of the mountains.

And said to the mountains and rocks, Fall on us, and hide us from the face of him that sits on the throne, and from the wrath of the Lamb;

For the great day of his wrath is come, and who shall be able to stand?

The above-mentioned verses from Matthew are quotes from Jesus, just after He has told the disciples about the abomination of desolation and the tribulation. He tells them that immediately after the tribulation, the sun and the moon will be darkened. This reference to the darkening of the sun and the moon is predicted in at least half a dozen places in the Bible: in Isaiah, Joel, Zachariah, Luke, and Revelation. The fact that it is mentioned so many times shows that it is a very important omen of change.

Obviously, for the sun to be darkened would require some catastrophic event. One that has been suggested is the eruption of many of the earth's 200 volcanoes within a very short length of time. This would throw so much dust and volcanic ash into the air that it would cause darkness at noon-day. This happened in some cities in Washington State when Mount St. Helens erupted.

The Revelation states that the moon will be as red as blood. Dust particles in the air diffract light, and this can cause the moon to appear red. Volcanic ash can also cause this effect. When a volcano on the island of Krakatoa exploded in the late 1800s, it set off a rash of sunset portraits in England because the particles released into the air created beautiful sunsets all over the world. Revelation states that the heavens will disappear like "a scroll when it is rolled together." This implies some type of smoke or dust cloud. When clouds roll in, they make the sky disappear in the same way a scroll disappears when it is rolled together.

Other possible causes for the darkening of the sun and moon are solar and lunar eclipses. These are the only times when we are used to the sun being darkened by the moon, and the moon being made red by being put in the earth's shadow. If the earth were to shift on its axis, then we would have solar and lunar eclipses that were not expected.

The possibility of a pole shift seems to be implied in Matthew 24 when it says that the "powers of the heavens will be shaken." What are the powers of heaven? In physics they are gravitation, rotation, and inertia. A pole shift would certainly shake these powers. Also Revelation says that "every mountain and island [will be] moved out of their places," an occurrence that would require a shift of the whole earth, causing volcanic eruptions and earthquakes. Interestingly enough, earthquakes can also throw up dust and make the sky darken. This occurred in the United States during the great Missouri quake of 1811.

After these earth changes occur, Jesus tells us that His sign will appear in heaven. His sign may be a cross or a star, like the star of Bethlehem. If it is the sign of the cross, it might be formed by planetary conjunctions or some other celestial phenomena. What the sign will be we cannot be certain, but the cross and the star of Bethlehem are Jesus' symbols.

The darkening of the sun and moon are the most important signs to look for before the Second Coming. As stated earlier, in terms of numbers this particular omen is mentioned in the Bible more than any other as a foreshadowing of the Second Coming – over a half dozen times in the Old and New Testaments.

Now let us turn to the Cayce readings and see what they have to say about the coming earth changes.

Q. Three hundred years ago Jacob Boehme decreed Atlantis would rise again at this crisis time when we cross from the Piscean Era into the Aquarian. Is Atlantis rising now? Will it cause a sudden convolution and about what year?

A. In 1998 we may find a great deal of the activities as have been wrought by the gradual changes that are coming about. These are at the periods when the cycle of the solar activity, or the years as related to the sun's passage through the various spheres of activity become paramount or [tantamount?] to the change between the Piscean and the Aquarian age. This is a gradual, not a cataclysmic activity in the experience of the earth in this period.   (1602-3)

As to the material changes that are to be as an omen, as a sign to those that this is shortly to come to pass – as has been given of old, the sun will be darkened and the earth shall be broken up in divers places – and THEN shall be PROCLAIMED – through the spiritual interception in the hearts and minds and souls of those that have sought His way – that HIS star has appeared, and will point the way for those that enter into the holy of holies in themselves. For, God the Father, God the Teacher, God the director, in the minds and hearts of men, must ever be IN those that come to know Him as first and foremost in the seeking of those souls; for He is first the GOD to the individual and as He is exemplified, as He is

manifested in the heart and in the acts of the
body, of the individual, He becomes manifested
before men. . .

As to the changes physical again: The earth will
be broken up in the western portion of America.
The greater portion of Japan must go into the sea.
The upper portion of Europe will be changed as
in the twinkling of an eye. Land will appear off the
east coast of America. There will be the upheavals
in the Arctic and in the Antarctic that will make
for the eruption of volcanoes in the Torrid areas,
and there will be shifting then of the poles – so
that where there has been those of a frigid or the
semi-tropical will become the more tropical, and
moss and fern will grow. And these will begin in
those periods in '58 to '98, when these will be proclaimed as the periods when His light will be seen
again in the clouds. As to times, as to seasons, as to
places, ALONE is it given to those who have
named the name – and who bear the mark of
those of His calling and His election in their bodies. To them it shall be given.   (3976-15)

In 3976-15 Cayce mentions the darkening of the sun
which is written about so often in the Bible. Also
mentioned along with this is the "breaking up" of the
earth by earthquakes, again, just as the Bible says. Reading
1602-3 seems to imply that the changes will be "gradual"
until 1998, when the greatest changes will occur. The
poles will ultimately be shifted, causing the weather to
change all over the world. In addition, upheavals in the
Arctic will cause volcanoes elsewhere to erupt, and Mount
St. Helens might be an example of this. All of these
changes will be in connection with a pole shift.

Volcanic eruptions have caused weather changes in the
past. In 1815 the Mount Tambora volcano in Indonesia

erupted and released so much dust into the atmosphere that the sun's rays were reflected, creating a very cool summer in North America. It was called the "year without a summer" because temperatures were still winterlike in the Northeast well into June. In 1982 the eruption of the Mexican volcano, El Chichon, caused a dust cloud that extended all the way around the world. Scientists immediately feared that the cloud would cool off the Earth's weather, especially since the cloud was situated at the equator, where the Earth gets most of its heat. Any major change in the Earth's weather could cause crop failure and lead to famine.

It has been discovered that the Earth's polar axis shifts a few feet every year. This shift was named the "Chandler wobble." It could be that this slight wobble in the axis could work its way into a major shift much in the same way that a slight wobble in a spinning top can accelerate it and cause it to fall over after a few turns.

According to Cayce, the last pole shift occurred 50,000 years ago. This information dovetails with evidence that has been found. In Siberia in the early 1900s, woolly mammoths were discovered frozen solid with summer food in their stomachs. Their bodies were so perfectly preserved that experts estimate only a quick freeze could have done the trick. Only a pole shift could have changed the weather so radically and so quickly that their bodies were frozen with no hint of decomposition. The radiocarbon dating of these mammoths put their deaths at between 44,000 and 48,000 B.C., the time period when Cayce says the last pole shift occurred. These mammoths were used by Immanuel Velikovski in his book, *Worlds in Collision*, as an example of past catastrophic earth changes.

In the previous earth-changes reading Cayce states that the sun's activity would become of "paramount" importance in this period of change. This could be a reference to the so-called sunspot cycle. Every eleven years the sun reverses polarity on its magnetic field. In between this eleven-year cycle is a five-and-one-half-year cycle of high and low activity in the sun's energy. The high activity is called the solar maximum. During the maximum year sunspot activity increases dramatically, and the weather on the earth warms up. During the minimum year the sunspots disappear, and the weather on the earth cools down. The time span between maximum and minimum years is not always five-and-one-half years but usually very close to it. During the last solar maximum year, 1980, the sun had the second highest number of spots ever recorded. This may have a had an effect on our activities and the earth itself.

Here is a list of the estimated solar peaks and valleys for the rest of the century: '80 maximum. '86 minimum. '91 maximum. '97 minimum.

In the latter part of the previous reading, Cayce states that changes will occur in America, Japan, and Europe. He states that the earth will be "broken up" in the western portion of America. Scientists for many years have said that the San Andreas fault in California was overdue for an earthquake, so any changes there would not come as a big surprise. Cayce also says that the "greater portion" of Japan must go into the sea. This fits perfectly with what geologists know about the nature of the earth's crust around Japan. This part of the crust (called a tectonic plate) is gradually dipping under another section of crust and is therefore called a subduction zone. Geologists believe this subduction will take millions of years, but Cayce seems to imply that it will happen much sooner. Although the reading does state that these changes will *begin* in the period '58 to '98, it does not say all these changes will happen before the end of this century. The phrase "changed as in the twinkling of an eye," however, suggests an immediate change for northern Europe. This could be the destruction of dikes in the Netherlands, which would flood a great deal of land in a very short time, since much of the Netherlands is below sea level. This comes to mind as the most vulnerable spot for earthquake destruction in Europe.

Part of this reading says that land will appear off the east coast of America. Cayce followers believe that this may have already happened with the birth of the volcanic island Surtsey in the Atlantic Ocean. If they are interpreting the reading correctly, part of Cayce's prophecy may have already been fulfilled. Surtsey rose right out of the ocean floor, formed by cooling lava, so in that sense it just "appeared."

Cayce gave another reading about earth changes that makes some very startling predictions about the changes that will occur in the United States:

> **As to conditions in the geography of the world, of the country – changes here are gradually coming about. No wonder, then, that the entity feels the need, the necessity for change of central location. For, many portions of the east coast will be disturbed, as well as many portions of the west coast, as well as the central portion of the U.S. In the next few years lands will appear in the Atlantic as well as in the Pacific. And what is the coast line now of many a land will be the bed of the ocean. Even many of the battle fields of the present will be ocean, will be the seas, the bays, the lands over which the NEW order will carry on their trade as one with another.**
>
> **Portions of the now east coast of New York, or New York City itself, will in the main disappear. This will be another generation, though, here; while the southern portions of Carolina, Georgia – these will disappear. This will be much sooner.**

The waters of the lakes will empty into the Gulf, rather than the waterway over which such discussions have been recently made. It would be well if the waterway were prepared, but not for that purpose for which it is at present being considered.

Then the area where the entity is now located [Virginia Beach] will be among the safety lands, as will be portions of what is now Ohio, Indiana and Illinois, and much of the southern portion of Canada and the eastern portion of Canada; while the western land – much of that is to be disturbed – in this land – as, of course, much in other lands. . .

Q. I have for many months felt that I should move away from New York City.

A. This is well, as indicated. There is too much unrest; there will continue to be the character of vibrations that to the body will be disturbing, and eventually those destruction forces there – though these will be in the next generation.

Q. Will Los Angeles be safe?

A. Los Angeles, San Francisco, most of all these will be among those that will be destroyed before New York even.

Q. Should California or Virginia Beach be considered at all, or where is the right place that God has already provided for me to live?

A. As indicated, these choices should be made rather in self. Virginia Beach or the area is much safer as a definite place. But the work of the entity should embrace most all of the areas from the east to the west coast, in its persuading – not as a preacher, nor as one bringing a message of doom, but as a loving warning to all groups, clubs, woman's clubs, writer's clubs, art groups, those of every form of club, that there needs be – in their activities – definite work towards the knowledge of the power of the Son of God's activity in the affairs of men. . .

Q. Is Virginia Beach to be safe?
A. It is the center – and the only seaport and center – of the White Brotherhood. (1152-11)

Again, as in the first reading we examined, Cayce says that the changes are coming about gradually. But in this reading he says that portions of the east coast will be disturbed as well as the west coast. He even predicts the destruction of New York City. What form this destruction will take is not spelled out, but the use of the word "disappear" seems to imply that it will be covered by the ocean. This disappearance is mentioned right after he says that the "coast line now of many a land" will be the bed of the ocean. Included in this submergence are the battlefields of World War II, which would include the coastlands of Europe. The oceans would only have to rise a few feet to cover much of what is now the coastland of many countries in Europe and elsewhere. Articles written in the past few years have stated that the burning of fossil fuels may cause the temperature of the earth to rise enough to make the polar ice caps melt. This would raise the ocean substantially and fulfill the prophecy.

There may be another cause of New York's destruction, however. Very few people are aware that there is an earthquake fault running right through the center of New York City. It is inactive at this time, but it might be activated by the earth changes.

Other changes are mentioned in this reading, including the disappearance of the southern portions of Georgia and the Carolinas. These areas, like New York City, are only a few feet above sea level and would be in danger of being covered by a rising ocean. In fact, southern Georgia and South Carolina were once the bottom of the ocean, and to this day have sandy soil from the deposits that occurred at that time.

One question we could ask is why would Virginia Beach be safe when other portions of the east coast will not? One possible reason is that the earth's crust around Virginia Beach is rising at the present time. During the last Ice Age the weight of the continental glacier that covered much of the United States caused the crust around Virginia Beach to sink, and the crust is just now recoiling from that sinkage. Perhaps during the earth changes whatever direction the earth's crust is heading will be accelerated, pushing Virginia Beach up even more.

Other safety areas mentioned are Indiana, Illinois, and southern and eastern Canada. This matches geological evidence, since Indiana and Illinois are very stable areas, and the rock crust in Canada is so hard that geologists refer to it as the "Canadian shield," the most geologically stable area in the world. This reading does state, however, that the waters of the Great Lakes will empty into the Gulf of Mexico, rather than the Atlantic via the St. Lawrence Seaway. Current geological trends show that the crust around the St. Lawrence Seaway is tilting back toward the Great Lakes and will one day cause the Lakes to empty into the Gulf. Geologists say that this will not happen for many thousands of years, but the trend may be accelerated by a pole shift.

The most disturbing part of this reading is that Cayce states that San Francisco and Los Angeles will be destroyed before New York. Given what we know about the earthquake activity in California, one does not have to be a psychic to predict this. Several major earthquakes occur each century along the San Andreas fault, and San

Francisco and Los Angeles are built dangerously close to the fault. Cayce states that the predictions for the destruction of these cities should be given as a "loving warning" and not as a "message of doom," but one must admit that these predictions are indeed gloomy.

For those who don't think major earth changes could occur in the central United States, consider the Missouri earthquake of December 16, 1811. It was the most powerful quake in United States history and was felt over a million square miles. It changed the course of the Mississippi River, creating new islands and lakes. Naturalist John J. Audubon stated that "the earth waved like a field of corn before the breeze." Eliza Bryan, a pioneer, described it as follows: "About 2 o'clock a.m. a violent shock of earthquake accompanied by a very awful noise resembling loud but distance thunder, but hoarse and vibrating, followed by complete saturation of the atmosphere with sulphurous vapor, causing total darkness." The Mississippi River actually stopped, rolled backward, and then surged ahead in huge tidal waves.

The most interesting point regarding this awesome destruction is that the earthquake caused total darkness. The sun's darkening predicted in the Bible may be caused by an earthquake as powerful.

Another interesting point about the earthquake in Missouri is that it created "earthquake Christians." People were so awestruck by the power of the quake and the threat of sudden death that they turned to religion. It has been said that "there are no atheists in foxholes," and apparently there are no atheists during earthquakes either.

Cayce tells us in the following reading that there will be a purpose behind the earth changes:

> **Ye say that these are of the sea; yes – for there shall the breaking up be, until there are those in every land that shall say that this or that shows the**

hand of divine interference, or that it is nature
taking a hand, or that it is the natural consequence
of good judgments.   (3976-26)

Cayce once again mentions the "breaking up" and says
that it will show the "hand of divine interference." One of
the Dead Sea Scrolls entitled the "Battle of the Sons of
Light and Darkness" speaks of the "Sons of Darkness"
being destroyed during the end time by a "hand not of
man." This might be a reference to the destruction of the
Anti-Christ by natural means such as an earthquake, much
as Jericho in the Bible was destroyed.

Of course, Cayce's comment on the "natural consequence of good judgments" is a reference to the building
of cities on earthquake faults – San Francisco and Los Angeles being the most obvious examples. Humanity should
know better than to build cities in seismically active areas,
for sooner or later a major quake will strike.

The destruction would seem inevitable even without the
coming earth changes. However, people through their
actions can have an effect on the earth. Exploding nuclear
devices underground and pumping oil out of the ground near
earthquake faults will cause the changes to be more severe.
We should realize this. On the positive side, Cayce repeatedly
stated that a small group of people praying together could
save a city, a state, or a region. He emphasized that some of
the predictions he made were trends, and that the will of
humankind could change the future. Cayce predicted earth
changes for northern Alabama in the 1930s that did not
occur, so it is probable that people in that area raised their
consciousness in such a way as to keep the destruction from
happening. Cayce has not been infallible in his predictions of
earth changes. Certainly the omens predicted in the Bible will
happen regardless of the actions of humans; however, we can
have an effect on our own destiny.

THE SECOND COMING

Up until now we have talked about the political and military events before the Second Coming, along with the preceding earth changes. But what about the Second Coming itself? Will Jesus come in the flesh? If so, where will the Second Coming take place? Once again, we will look at what the Bible and the Cayce readings say about these questions. Surprisingly, they are relatively easy questions to answer.

The following section of the Bible describes Jesus' ascension into heaven after the resurrection:

Acts 1:9-12

And when he had spoken these things, while they beheld, he was taken up, and a cloud received him out of their sight.

And while they looked steadfastly toward heaven as he went up, behold, two men stood by them in white apparel;

Who also said, men of Galilee, why do you stand

gazing up into heaven? This same Jesus, who is taken up from you into heaven, shall so come in like manner as you have seen him go into heaven.

Then they returned to Jerusalem from the Mount called Olives which is from Jerusalem a sabbath day's journey.

Jesus ascends from the top of Mount Olives into heaven, and is received by a cloud. Two men in white standing alongside tell the men of Galilee that Jesus will return "in like manner." The phrase, "in like manner," literally means in exactly the same manner. This means that Jesus will return to Mount Olives, descending exactly as He ascended. Mount Olives is very close to Jerusalem, and the appearance of Jesus there will be seen all over the city; thus His reappearance will be apparent to all the world.

To those familiar with the Bible His appearance will be anticipated. Now let's look at what Cayce says about the Second Coming:

Q. Is Jesus the Christ on any particular sphere or is He manifesting on the earth plane in another body?

A. As just given, all power in heaven, in earth, is given to Him who overcame. Hence He is of Himself in space, in the force that impels through faith, through belief, in the individual entity. As a Spirit Entity. Hence not in a body in the earth, but may come at will to him who WILLS to be one with, and acts in love to make same possible. For, He shall come as ye have seen Him go, in the BODY He occupied in Galilee. The body that He formed, that was crucified on the cross, that rose from the tomb, that walked by the sea, that appeared to Simon, that appeared to Philip, that appeared to "I, even John."   (5749-4)

The first part of this reading has to do with Jesus as a spirit entity. Cayce tells us that anyone can be with the Christ spirit if he or she desires and acts in love to make it possible.

The second part of this reading deals with the physical return of Jesus and even quotes a translation of the verses of Acts we just looked at, stating that Jesus will return even as the men of Galilee saw Him go. So Cayce agrees with the Bible that Jesus will return in the flesh to Mount Olives. He will occupy the same body He did before, the body that was crucified and rose from the tomb. He will be recognized as Jesus, and so Cayce is definitely speaking of a physical return. These next readings emphasize this point even more:

> *Q. What is meant by "the day of the Lord is near at hand"?*
>
> **A. That as has been promised through the prophets and the sages of old, the time – and half time – has been and is being fulfilled in this day and generation. . .**
>
> *Q. How soon?*
>
> **A. When those that are His have made the way clear, PASSABLE, for Him to come.   (262-49)**
>
> **Keep the faith that ye are magnified in the Persian experience, as ye sought for Him who is the light, the hope of the world today. For until there is again the seeking of such as ye not only proclaimed but manifested, he CANNOT come again.   (1908-1)**

The quote from the Bible Book of Acts is once again emphasized. Another point is added: Jesus cannot come again until those that are "His" have made the way passable. This point is explained in reading 1908-1 by the fact that there must be the seeking of the Christ Spirit before Jesus will return. This seeking will be the attracting principle that will bring Jesus back to earth. Like attracts like. This is explained in the following readings:

Q. He said He would come again. What about His second coming?

A. The time no one knows. Even as He gave, not even the Son Himself. ONLY the Father. Not until His enemies – and the earth – are wholly in subjection to His will. His powers.

Q. Are we entering the period of preparation for His coming?

A. Entering the test period, rather.   (5749-2)

Q. When Jesus the Christ comes the second time, will He set up His kingdom on earth and will it be an everlasting kingdom?

A. Read His promises in that ye have written of His words, even as "I gave." He shall rule for a thousand years. Then shall Satan be loosed again for a season.   (5749-4)

Q. Please explain what is meant by "He will walk and talk with men of every clime." Does this mean He will appear to many at once or appear to various people during a long period?

A. As given, for a thousand years He will walk and talk with men of every clime. Then in groups, in masses, and then they shall reign of the first resurrection for a thousand years; for this will be when the changes materially come. . .

Q. In the Persian experience as San (or Zend) did Jesus give the basic teachings of what became Zoroastrianism?

A. In all those periods that the basic principle was the Oneness of the Father, He has walked with men.   (364-8)

He will not tarry, for having overcome He shall appear even AS the Lord AND Master. Not as one born, but as one that returneth to His own, for He will walk and talk with men of every clime, and those that are faithful and just in their reckoning shall be caught up with Him to rule and to do JUDGMENT for a thousand years!   (364-7)

We can see from these readings that Jesus will not return until the whole earth is in subjection to His will. This is certainly not the case today, and it will take a powerful stimulus for this to occur. But once again, Cayce states that the earth must be ready for Him if He is to return. I believe the key to this change in consciousness by the people of the earth will be the darkening of the sun. It is one of the most important omens – mentioned repeatedly in the Bible as preceding the Second Coming. It is written in the Koran, so it will be recognized universally as proof of His coming. Signs such as this will be so incredible that people all over the earth will have only one place to turn for help, to God. The power of millions of people praying will create an attraction that will draw Jesus back to the earth.

The test period mentioned in 5749-2 is happening right at this moment. All of us are being tried on our willingness to subject our will to the will of God. This is the test.

Mentioned in all four of the previous readings is the thousand years of peace that will follow the Second Coming. This is referred to as the "millennium" by the fundamentalists and the "Age of Aquarius" by the New Age people. It will be a period of time unparalleled in human history. Evil will be set aside, and peace among humankind will be the rule. It is written about in the Book of Revelation in the following verses:

Revelation 20:2-4

And he laid hold on the dragon, that old serpent

who is the Devil and Satan, and bound him a thousand years.

And cast him into the bottomless pit, and shut him up, and set a seal upon him, that he should deceive the nations no more, till the thousand years should be fulfilled; and after that he must be loosed a little season.

And I saw thrones, and they sat upon them, and judgment was given to them; and I saw the souls of them that were beheaded for the witness of Jesus, and for the word of God, and who had not worshiped the beast, neither his image, neither had received his mark upon their foreheads, or in their hands; and they lived and reigned with Christ a thousand years.

Satan will be locked up for a thousand years, after which time he will be released for a season. Those allowed to incarnate during this time will be only those who have not worshiped the animal influences. All will realize and accept the existence of God. There will be no more war or hatred. In short, this will be the greatest time in human history.

Let's look at the common points of agreement between the Bible and the Cayce readings. Both agree that there will be a physical return of Jesus at Mount Olives. Both say that this event will be preceded by the sun being darkened and the appearance of an Anti-Christ (Cayce says a "Xerxes"). Cayce clarifies this even further by stating that we are going through a testing period at the present time. Finally, Cayce tells us that the entrance of the Messiah in this period will be in 1998.

Given Cayce's date of 1998 and all the events mentioned in the Bible, we can produce the following chart:

1991 "Confirming the covenant with many"
     The Middle East Peace Conference
     Temple Mount in Jerusalem is desecrated
     Israel is invaded
     Beginning of the tribulation
1998 The sun and the moon are darkened
     The Second Coming at Mount Olives
     Beginning of the millennium

The only events in question in this chart are the desecration of the Temple Mount, the invasion of Israel, and the beginning of the tribulation. As time goes on, it seems more and more likely that they will occur at the end of the seven-year period, in 1998.

At the end of the tribulation the sun will be darkened as an omen of the beginning of the New Age. This will occur in 1998. Then Jesus will return to Mount Olives, and the millennium will begin.

Cayce gave the following readings to inspire those who might doubt the reality of the Second Coming:

. . .leave not out of thy faith nor thy hope those purposes that should be the promptings of this individual entity. For when ye walk with Him, in purpose and in ideal, ye will find that ye are never alone. Think not that ye or any other individual may be the only one serving a living God. For since His entry into the world, and His making it possible for man to find his way back to God, there has been and will continue to be an increase. For God has not willed that any soul should perish. Though the lights of hope may oft grow dim, in the violence that is created by those who become self-conscious of ability and who use self and others for gratifying of selfish desires, let it ever be said of thee that ye will make, ye will cause the welkin to ring for the glory of the coming of the Lord. For

He will one day come again, and thou shalt see
Him as He is, even as thou hast seen in thy early
sojourns the glory of the day of the triumphal entry
and the day of the Crucifixion, and as ye also heard
the angels proclaim "As ye have seen Him go, so
will ye see Him come again." Thou wilt be among
those in the earth when He comes again. Glory in
that, but let it be rather the one reason why ye
keep the faith, the faith in the coming of the Lord,
to call those who have been faithful; that they, as
He prayed, "may be where I am, and may behold
the glory which I had with thee before the worlds
were."   (3615-1)

*Q. . . .For some time I have been thinking con-
tinually about the coming of the Kingdom on earth
and His coming. Has it any bearing upon the lesson?
Please give me more light upon the Kingdom and
His coming.*

A. How long has been the cry of those that
have manifested in the earth the glory of the Father through the Son, "Hasten, O Lord, the day
of thy kingdom in the earth!" How have the
promises read that the Son has given? "I go to
prepare a place that where I am there ye may be
also. I will come again and receive you unto my-
self." Then, as the individual heart attunes its
mind and its body-activity into that consciousness of the desire for the hastening of that day.
Yet the merciful kindness of the Father has, in
the eyes of many, delayed the coming, and many
have cried even as the parable He gave, "We
know not what has become of this man. Show us
other gods that may lead us in this day." Yet the
cry in the heart and the soul of those that seek
His way is to hasten that day. Yet, as He has
given, in patience, in listening, in being still, may
ye know that the Lord doeth all things well. Be

not weary that He apparently prolongs His time, for – as the Master has given, "As to the day, no man knoweth, not even the son, but the Father and they to whom the Father may reveal the Son prepareth the way that all men may know the love of the Father." And as ye would be the channel to hasten that glorious day of the coming of the Lord, then do with a might that thy hands find to do to make for the greater manifestations of the love of the Father in the earth. For, into thy keeping, and to His children and to His sons, has he committed the keeping of the saving of the world, of the souls of men; for, as He has given, "Who is my mother? Who is my brother? Who is my sister? They that do the will of my Father who is in heaven, the same is my mother, my brother, my sister." So, as He gave, "I leave thee, but I will come again and receive as many as ye have quickened through the manifesting in thy life the will of the Father in the earth." Hence, know that, as thine mind, thine activities, long more and more for the glorifying of the Son in the earth, for the coming of the day of the Lord, He draws very nigh unto thee.   (262-58)

When I speak of possible dates for the Second Coming, people invariably quote the Bible verse just mentioned, "As to the day, no man knoweth," and say that no one can know the time or the day. But Cayce goes a little further with this and says that it may be revealed by God. I believe that God has revealed the year 1998 to Edgar Cayce and to us through his readings. I also believe that as the time draws near for this event, the timing will become even more clear to all of us. Humankind was meant to understand and can always learn more through an inquiring mind, and I believe we are meant to know the timing of these important events.

A Physical Description of Jesus

When Jesus returns, how will we know Him? What will He look like? Unknown to most people there is a physical description of Jesus in the archives of Rome. This description is contained in a report written two thousand years ago by a Roman, Publius Lentulus, to the Emperor Tiberias:

"There has appeared in Palestine a man who is still living and whose power is extraordinary. He has the title given him of Great Prophet; his disciples call him the Son of God. He raises the dead and heals all sorts of diseases.

"He is a tall, well-proportioned man, and there is an air of severity in his countenance which at once attracts the love and reverence of those who see him. His hair is the color of new wine from the roots to the ears, and thence to the shoulders, it is curled and falls down to the lowest part of them. Upon the forehead, it parts in two after the manner of Nazarenes.

"His forehead is flat and fair, his face without blemish or defect, and adorned with a graceful expression. His nose and mouth are very well proportioned, his beard is thick and the color of his hair. His eyes are gray and extremely lively.

"In his reproofs, he is terrible, but his exhortations and instructions, amiable and courteous. There is something wonderfully charming in his face with a mixture of gravity. He is never seen to laugh, but has been observed to weep [Cayce says he did laugh and quite often]. He is very straight in stature, his hands large and spreading, his arms are very beautiful. He talks little, but with a great quality and is the handsomest man in the world."

The description of Jesus in the Cayce readings agrees with the one above:

> . . .a vision of the Master as might be put on canvas. . . [would] be entirely different from all these which have been depicted of the face, the body, the eyes, the cut of the chin and the lack entirely of the Jewish or Aryan profile. For these were clear, clean, ruddy, hair almost like that of David, a golden brown, yellow-red. . . (5354-1)

> The Master's hair is 'most red, inclined to be curly in portions, yet not feminine or weak – STRONG, with heavy piercing eyes that are blue or steel-gray. (5749-1)

In other readings we are told that Jesus wore a pearl gray robe. So a complete picture Jesus would be of a tall, well-proportioned man wearing a pearl gray robe and having reddish brown hair and steel-gray eyes. This is what Jesus will look like when He returns.

THE LAST JUBILEE SCROLL

In 1947 two Bedouin shepherds were tending their flocks by the northwest shores of the Dead Sea. One of their goats wandered into a nearby cave, and one of the shepherds tossed in a rock to chase the wayward goat out. The rock apparently shattered something, because the sound of breaking pottery was heard. The Bedouin entered the cave to discover what had been broken. He found eight jars (one broken), and in one of the jars he found seven antique scrolls. Thinking they might be valuable, he eventually took them to an antique dealer in Jerusalem and offered to sell the scrolls for twenty pounds. The dealer refused, thinking the price too high, and the Bedouin took the scrolls to another dealer who bought them. Ultimately, the scrolls were discovered to be two thousand years old and were undoubtedly the most sensational archaeological find of this century. They, along with the other scrolls that were discovered later in the same area, became known as the Dead Sea Scrolls.

The discovery of the scrolls set off much archaeological

activity in the area of Qumran, not far from where they were discovered. A group of ruins was excavated about a mile from the cave where the first scrolls were found. Coins found in the ruins were dated from 125 B.C. to 68 A.D. From this and other evidence archaeologists decided that the writers of the scrolls lived in this community and put the scrolls in the caves to save them from the Roman invasion of Palestine in 68 A.D.

Much debate began about who the people of the Qumran community were. Because the scrolls were Hebrew scriptures including the Book of Isaiah, the community was obviously a Hebrew sect. Most scholars now believe that the people who occupied the community of Qumran were members of a pious monastic group known as the Essenes. The rules of conduct printed in the scrolls were essentially Essene, and the ancient historian Pliny places an Essene community at the exact location of the Qumran ruins on the Dead Sea. From this evidence most scholars are now convinced that the scrolls were the property of the Essenes.

Most of what we know about the Essenes comes to us from the first-century historian Josephus. The Essenes were a puritan community of which one could not be a member without passing rigorous tests. The trial period was three years, at which time the community would decide whether the prospective member could join. At the time of joining, a member turned all property over to the members of the sect to be shared equally.

The Essenes participated in strict religious discipline. Some members of the sect did not believe in marriage and rejected all sexual conduct. Others believed in marriage as necessary for continuation of life, and all believed in the controlling of passions as necessary for a spiritual life. As part of this life, they arose before sunrise and before dealing with the matters of the day, joined in joyous prayers as the sun rose. They prayed before and after meals, and lived a life of dedication today only associated with monasteries.

The importance of the Essenes to us is their close association with John the Baptist and later with Jesus. Water was one of the Essenes' most important symbols and John, as an Essene, incorporated it into his name. Other than the baptismal ritual of John, the Essenes believed in bathing every day, something that was very unusual at that time. Of course, the most famous baptism by John was the baptism of Jesus. This connects Jesus with the Essenes because baptism was definitely an Essene ritual. Equally strong evidence is found in the fact that the baptism occurred in an area not far from the Essene community. There is no doubt, however, that John was much more the Essene than Jesus, for John believed in the letter of the law, while Jesus was the embodiment of the spirit of the law.

The following paragraph from the historian Josephus gives us an idea of just what type of people the Essenes were:

"And truly, as for other things, they do nothing but according to the injunctions of their curators; only these two things are done among them at every one's own free will, which are, to assist those that want it, and to show mercy; for they are permitted of their own accord to afford succor to such as deserve it, when they stand in need of it, and to bestow food on those that are in distress: but they cannot give anything to their kindred without the curators. They dispense their anger after a just manner, and restrain their passion. They are eminent for fidelity, and rate the ministers of peace; whatsoever they say also is firmer than an oath; but swearing is avoided by them, and they esteem it worse than perjury; for they say that he who cannot be believed without

swearing by God is already condemned. They also take great pains in studying the writings of the ancients, and choose out of them what is most for the advantage of their soul and body. . ." *

This is the traditional historical view of the Essenes. The Edgar Cayce readings give a different view, making them much more important in the life of Jesus than traditional history would have us believe.

Cayce tells us that the Essenes were a mystical brotherhood organized for the specific purpose of paving the way for the entrance of Christ into the world. The Essenes' purpose was to purify themselves in order to prepare a virgin who would be a pure channel for the birth of the Christ Child. The readings say that the word Essene means "expectancy," namely, the expectant birth of the Christ Child.

Twelve young girls were chosen as possible channels for the birth, Mary being one of the twelve. Not that the Essenes would choose the girl, but that they might help provide a group from which God would choose one to be the channel for the birth. This would involve an attraction principle much in the same way that the subjection of the whole earth to His Will will attract Jesus the second time. A pure enough channel would attract the spirit of Jesus. As Mary climbed the steps to the altar during the Essene's sunrise worship one day, an angel appeared to the congregation and announced that Mary was the chosen one. Later, after the birth when the Holy Family fled into Egypt, members of the Essenes provided protection and guidance along the journey.

What does all this have to do with prophecy? The Essenes were a very spiritual group closely associated with Jesus during the time of His entrance to the earth plane in

*Flavius Josephus, *Selections from His Works*, Abraham Wasserstein, Viking Press, New York.

the first century. They knew of the entrance of Jesus ahead of time and, according to Josephus, were renowned for their ability to prophesy the future.

Is it possible, then, that the Dead Sea Scrolls, written by Essene prophets, could apply to the Second Coming of Jesus? The Essenes were very familiar with the cycles of the ages and believed that each change in the cycle was accompanied by great changes within the earth. It is possible that some of the Essenes had visions of the distant future. It seems an incredible coincidence that the discovery of the Dead Sea Scrolls occurred at the exact time Israel was being founded (1947-'48). Perhaps these scrolls were meant to be found during this time to give us a greater understanding of the past and the future.

With this possibility in mind we will examine one of the Dead Sea Scrolls entitled "The Last Jubilee." (I have chosen three sections of the Scroll, rather than the entire Scroll, which is of some length.) The Scroll is about the "Last Days" during which time it says, a "Melchizedek redivivus" (reincarnate) will appear and destroy Belial (Satan) and lead the children of God to eternal forgiveness:

The Last Jubilee Scroll

"When, therefore, the scripture speaks of a Day of Atonement to be observed in the seventh month, on the tenth day of that month what is meant, in an eschatological sense, is that this final Jubilee will be marked by a day on which all the children of light and all who have cast their lot with the cause of righteousness will achieve forgiveness of their sins, whereas the wicked will reap their deserts and be brought to an end. . .

"There is a further reference to this final judgment in the continuation of the verse from the psalter. How long, we read, will you go judging unjustly and showing partiality to the wicked? Selah. The allusion is to Belial and the spirits of his ilk – that is, to elders who sit in assides but defy God's statutes in order to perfect justice. The future king of righteousness – that is, Melchizedek redivivus – will execute upon them God's avenging judgment, and at the same time deliver the just from the hands of Belial and all those spirits of his ilk. With all the angels of righteousness at his aid, he will blast the council of Belial to destruction. But the faithful, as the Psalmist says, will return to their eminence, the eminence in question being the destination of all who are indeed children of God.

"At that time, it will be from Belial, not from God, that men will turn away in rebellion, and there will be a re-establishment of the reign of righteousness, perversity being confounded by the judgments of God. This is what scripture implies in the words, 'Who says to Zion, your God has not claimed his kingdom!' The term zion there denoting the total congregation of the 'sons of righteousness,' that is, those who maintain the covenant and turn away from the popular trend, and your God signifying the king of righteousness, alias Melchizedek redivivus, who will destroy Belial.

"Our text speaks also of sounding a loud trumpet blast throughout the land on the tenth day of the seventh month. As applied to the last days, this refers to the fanfare which will then be sounded before the messianic king."*

Melchizedek was a priest described in the Bible as an eternal being. It says that he had no "beginning of days" and no end of life, that is, he was not born of woman and did not die but ascended into heaven.

The Cayce readings tell us that Melchizedek was a

*The Dead Sea Scriptures, Theodor H. Gaster, Anchor Books, Garden City, N.Y., 1976.

previous incarnation of Jesus. The Book of Hebrews supports this when it says that Jesus was a "priest after the order of Melchizedek." This Melchizedek-Jesus link is very important because if Melchizedek was a previous incarnation of Jesus, then this scroll could be describing the Second Coming of Jesus, the *Melchizedek redivivus* (reincarnate).

A "Jubilee" is the fiftieth year of a fifty-year period which has special significance for the Jews. This fiftieth year begins on the tenth day of the seventh month. This is the day designated each year as the Day of Atonement, the holiest day of the year for the Jews. The writer of the "Last Jubilee" believed this fifty-year period would conclude with the arrival of a messianic king on the Day of Atonement.

The state of Israel was founded in 1948. The Cayce readings state that the Second Coming will occur in 1998. Could this last Jubilee be the fifty-year period of the existence of Israel before the Second Coming? (1948 + 50 = 1998) Certainly the Second Coming would fit the description of a "final judgment" in the Last Jubilee Scroll.

The Jubilee year in the Jewish calendar is what is known as a sabbatical year. A sabbatical year occurs every seven years, but only every seventh sabbatical year is a Jubilee year. During the sabbatical year, Jews are not supposed to plant crops or collect debts. They are supposed to release their debtors of all debts and release all captives which they might have. The sabbatical year was of such great importance to the Jews that the failure to observe it caused them to be led into the Babylonian captivity.

The following section of Leviticus describes the sabbatical year:

Leviticus 25:8-12

And you shall number seven sabbaths of years to you, seven times seven years; and the space of the

seven sabbaths of years shall be to you forty and nine years.

Then shall you cause the trumpet of the Jubilee to sound on the tenth day of the seventh month, in the Day of Atonement shall you make the trumpet sound throughout all your land.

And you shall hallow the fiftieth year, and proclaim liberty throughout all the land to all the inhabitants thereof; it shall be a jubilee to you; and you shall return every man to his possession, and you shall return every man to his family.

A jubilee shall that fiftieth year be to you; you shall not sow, neither reap that which grows of itself in it, nor gather in it the grapes of your vine unpruned.

For it is the jubilee, it shall be holy to you; you shall eat the increase thereof out of the field.

The Jubilee year or any other sabbatical year does not begin until the first day of the seventh month of the religious year. This is because the religious year begins in the spring, but the secular year does not begin until the first day of the seventh month of the religious calendar. This is confusing, so just think of the first day of the seventh month as the Jewish New Year.

There are three Jewish holidays in the fall during this seventh month. They are the Feast of the Trumpets, first day of the seventh month; Day of Atonement, tenth day of the seventh month; and the Feast of Tabernacles, fifteenth day of the seventh month. The Day of Atonement is the only day of the year when the high priest enters the holy of holies in the temple and sprinkles the blood of the sacrifice on the mercy seat of the ark of the covenant. This fact is very important to the evidence we are going to look at in support of our theory about the Scroll. The symbolism of the Day of Atonement will provide much of the background we will examine.

Even more important than this, however, is the trumpet blast that begins each fiftieth Jubilee year Day of Atonement. This can be seen from Jesus' description of the Second Coming in Matthew 24:30-31:

> **And there shall appear the sign of the Son of man in heaven; and then shall all the tribes of the earth mourn, and they shall see the Son of man coming in the clouds of heaven with power and great glory.**
>
> **And he shall send his angels with a great sound of a trumpet, and they shall gather together his elect from the four winds from one end of heaven to the other.**

As Jesus returns to the earth, there will be the sound of a trumpet blast. Could this be the trumpet blast of the Last Jubilee? This would mean that the Second Coming would occur on the Day of Atonement in the fall of 1998. Thus, from the Last Jubilee Scroll and the prophecies of Edgar Cayce, we may know the date of the Second Coming.

So far we have seen that the fifty-year period of the state of Israel and Cayce's date for the Second Coming are the same, and that both the Jubilee year and the Second Coming begin with a trumpet blast. These facts by themselves could be merely a coincidence. But there is more evidence.

The Book of Revelation is primarily concerned with future events relating to the Second Coming. In chapters 8-11 these events are symbolized by seven trumpets. I believe these trumpets could stand for the seven years of Daniel's seven-year period. Since each secular Jewish New Year begins with the Feast of the Trumpets, the seven trumpets could symbolize seven years. Most important to us, however, is that when the seventh trumpet sounds in Revelation 11, the temple of God is opened up, and the Ark of the Covenant is seen. The only time the Ark of the Covenant is seen in the temple in Jerusalem is on the Day of Atonement. So, the sounding of the seventh trumpet (which symbolizes the Second Coming) is related to the Day of Atonement, not only through the trumpet blast but through the viewing of the Ark of the Covenant. And this is not the only connection between the Day of Atonement and Jesus. The Book of Hebrews relates the two very strongly in the following verses:

Hebrews 9:7-12

But into the second [holy of holies] went the high priest alone once every year, not without blood, which he offered for himself, and for the errors of the people. The Holy [Spirit] thus signifying that the way into the holiest of all was not yet made manifest, while the first tabernacle was yet standing. Which was a figure for the time then present, in which were offered both gifts and sacrifices that could not make him that did the service perfect, as pertaining to the conscience; Which stood only in foods, and drinks, and various washings, and carnal ordinances, imposed on them until the time of reformation. But Christ being come as high priest of good things to come, by a greater and more perfect tabernacle, not made with hands, that is to say, not of this building. Neither by the blood of goats and calves, but by his own blood he entered in once into the holy place, having obtained eternal redemption for us.

The writer of the Hebrews explains to us that once a year the high priest enters the holy of holies to offer calves' blood for the sins of the Jewish people. Jesus, when He came, made this unnecessary by "His perfect tabernacle,"

His body and spirit. By "His own blood" Jesus entered the holy place in heaven – not in the temple.

This shows that Jesus' crucifixion was symbolically related to the Day of Atonement. This symbolism is so strong that at the moment Jesus died on the cross, the veil in the temple that separated the holy place from the holy of holies was torn in two (Matthew 27:51). Jesus opened the way for all humankind to enter the holy of holies within themselves through prayer and meditation. This tearing of the veil at the crucifixion connects Jesus directly with the Day of Atonement, since the veil is passed only on that day.

The ninth chapter of Daniel is one of the key chapters in the Bible dealing with Second Coming prophecy. Verse 24 of that chapter states that "seventy weeks" (or years) are determined "to make an end to iniquity"; this "end" occurs at the time of the coming of the Messiah. The phrase that is translated "make an end to iniquity" literally means "atone for sins." The Hebrew word used is *Kaphar* which means "atone for." This statement that at the time of the Second Coming all sins will be atoned for could be interpreted as a reference to the Day of Atonement.

Another important perspective in this is the way great events in Jewish history have revolved around the high holy days of autumn. When the Jews left captivity in Babylon and began to return to Jerusalem, their main goal was to rebuild the temple and reestablish the ritual sacrifice and worship. When the sacrifice was restored, it was begun on the first day of the seventh month, the Jewish New Year. Many years later a revival under Ezra was begun on the same day. Two thousand years later in 1973, a war between the Arabs and Israelis was fought on the Day of Atonement and thus named the Yom Kippur (Day of Atonement) War.

The Jewish New Year in 1998 falls on September 20. The Day of Atonement 1998 begins at sundown on the

29th of September and ends at sundown on the 30th of
September. This may be the day people have waited for,
for two thousand years. It will be exciting to see if the
writer of the Last Jubilee Scroll was correct about the
return of the King of Righteousness on the Day of
Atonement.

We have been examining Bible verses, so far, for
evidence of a Second Coming during the high holy days in
1998, but is there any clue about such an event in the
Cayce readings? I think so. Read through this reading we
have seen before:

> **As to the material changes that are to be as an
> omen, as a sign to those that this is shortly to come
> to pass – as has been given of old, the sun will be
> darkened and the earth shall be broken in divers
> places – and THEN shall be PROCLAIMED –
> through the spiritual interception in the hearts and
> minds and souls of those that have sought His way
> – that HIS star has appeared, and will point the way
> for those that enter into the holy of holies in
> themselves.   (3976-15)**

The phrase "the holy of holies in themselves" refers to
those who pray and meditate. What is interesting is that
Cayce chose to use this phrase in referring to the period of
time after the sun is darkened. It is clear from Matthew 24
that the Second Coming will occur immediately after the
darkening of the sun, and it is here that Cayce mentions
the holy of holies. This could be interpreted as an oblique
reference to the Day of Atonement.

Another possible Cayce reference to a Day of Atonement Second Coming comes in a reading we examined
earlier. When asked what the purpose of World War II
was, Cayce told the person to read the 31st chapter of
Deuteronomy, and "we will see." (257-211) Part of this
chapter has to do with the return of the Jews to the Holy

Land. In addition, there are two verses that are as follows:

Deuteronomy 31:10-11

And Moses commanded them, saying, At the end of every seven years, in the solemnity of the year of release. in the Feast of Tabernacles, When all Israel is come to appear before the Lord your God in the place which he shall choose, you shall read this law before all Israel in their hearing.

The time mentioned in these verses is the 15th day of the seventh month, right at the beginning of the sabbatical year. As every Jubilee year is a sabbatical year, this would point to the possibility of the year being a Jubilee year. And since the Feast of Tabernacles is only five days after the Day of Atonement, Cayce could be referring to a future Jubilee. This may be stretching the point a bit, but it does fit with all the other evidence.

The final Bible chapter in this web of evidence is Zachariah 14. It mentions the return of Jesus to Mount Olives, and a battle involving many nations for Jerusalem.

The part that interests us has to do with the Feast of the Tabernacles and the time period after the Second Coming. It reads as follows:

Zachariah 14:16-19

And it shall come to pass that every one that is left of all the nations which came against Jerusalem shall even go up from year to year to worship the King, the Lord of hosts, and to keep the Feast of Tabernacles. And it shall be that whoever will not come up of all the families of the earth to Jerusalem to worship the King, the Lord of hosts, even upon them shall be no rain. And if the family of Egypt go not up, and come not, that have no rain, there shall be the plague, with which the Lord will smite the

nations that come not up to keep the Feast of Tabernacles. This shall be the punishment of Egypt, and the punishment of all nations that come not up to keep the Feast of Tabernacles.

The important thing to keep in mind is that these verses are describing events *after* the Second Coming. The verses previous to these have set the stage by describing the events of the Second Coming. Now Zachariah is telling us that during the millennium any country that does not come to Jerusalem to celebrate the Feast of Tabernacles will not find favor in God's sight. Why would the people of the world be celebrating an essentially Jewish holiday *after* the Second Coming? Could it be that they will be celebrating an event that coincides with the Feast of the Tabernacles? If the Second Coming is on the Day of Atonement, then the Feast of Tabernacles might be the date used to celebrate, since it is only five days after the Day of Atonement. There would be no need to have a Day of Atonement anymore, since as Hebrews has told us, Jesus substituted His blood on the cross for the blood of the sacrifice sprinkled on the holy of holies. To me it makes no sense for people to be celebrating the Feast of Tabernacles after the Second Coming unless the Second Coming itself occurred around the same time of year.

An interesting phenomenon has begun to appear in recent years in Jerusalem, and *Time* magazine describes it as follows:

> **"As the end of the world nears, according to the biblical prophet Zachariah, visitors from many nations will gather each year in Jerusalem to worship the king, the Lord almighty, and to celebrate the Feast of Tabernacles. These words took life last week (October 1981) as 3,000 people from 35 countries celebrated tabernacles, or**

sukkoth, with parades, cookouts, and musical services in one of the holy city's most spectacular religious events of the year. Significantly, the celebrants were Christians."

Fascinating, isn't it? Christians have already begun to celebrate the Feast of Tabernacles! *Time* says of the people involved, "Virtually all are millennarians who believe that Zionism is part of God's design for the days preceding the Second Coming of Jesus Christ." Already it seems that preparations are being made for the Second Coming.

Now to review some of the key points of this chapter:

1. The Last Jubilee Scroll tells us that a Melchizedek (reincarnate) will return on the Day of Atonement during a Jubilee year (fiftieth) to destroy evil and establish righteousness.

   The Edgar Cayce readings say that Melchizedek was a previous incarnation of Jesus.

2. The Jewish state was founded in 1948, so its Jubilee year will be 1998.

   The Edgar Cayce readings say that Jesus will return in 1998.

3. The Last Jubilee Scroll says that the Melchizedek redivivus's return will be accompanied by a trumpet blast.

   Jesus tells us that His return will be accompanied by a trumpet blast.

All the evidence we have looked at aside, no one can state for certain when the Second Coming will be. As the Bible says "as to the day and the hour no man knoweth save the Father." This does not keep us from speculating, however.

September 30, 1998

I have been an astrologer for over twenty years, so when I realized the implications of the Last Jubilee Scroll, the first thing I did was run to my ephemeris to check out the astrological aspects for the Day of Atonement, 1998. What I found was amazing! If you were to pick a day in 1998 for the Second Coming, the Day of Atonement is the perfect day astrologically.

Before we look at the astrological aspects for the Day of Atonement in 1998, however, I want to go through a brief explanation of how astrology works.

Edgar Cayce tells us that the Magi who attended the birth of Jesus were astrologers. In fact, the word *Magi* is the Greek word for astrologer or "one who studies the stars."

Cayce was asked how the Magi knew about the birth of Jesus. Cayce said they knew through the psychic and the astrological. Because of this I believe we can be like latter-day Magi. We have the psychic with Edgar Cayce, and we have the astrological with the Day of Atonement, 1998.

Edgar Cayce gave one-word explanations for the planets and their influences. They are:

Mercury – mind	Saturn – change
Venus – love	Uranus – extremes
Earth – flesh	Neptune – mystic
Mars – madness	Pluto – consciousness
Jupiter – strength	

I want you to keep these definitions in mind when you look at the astrological charts in this chapter.

To the lay person astrology seems very complicated. But to me astrology is like the legal profession. The more complicated it is, the more they can charge to interpret it. To me astrology is very simple. All of astrology can be broken down into two simple facts, and they are that 90- and 180-degree aspects are bad, and 60- and 120-degree aspects are good.

That's all there is to astrology. Everything else is just stuff that astrologers have piled on to make it more complicated.

As astrologers, what we try to look for are patterns of planets in 60- and 120-degree aspects or 90- and 180-degree aspects. When you have a large number of planets in 60- and 120-degree aspects, the influence is good. When you have a large number of planets in 90- and 180-degree aspects, the influence is bad. At these times the events that are occurring on the earth will be good or bad depending on the aspects.

I want to show you a couple of astrological charts from the past, and how the astrological aspects fit with the events that were happening on the earth during those time periods. Then we will look at the charts for 1998.

Cayce gave a reading in the spring of 1941 in which he said that the astrological aspects for that time were very unusual. He said that it was a time when the forces of light and darkness were battling on the earth. This can be seen very easily by looking at the astrological aspects for May 10, 1941.

On that day there was a huge conjunction of the sun and the planets, Mercury, Venus, Jupiter, Saturn, and Uranus in the sign of Taurus. These were all in bad aspect with Mars and the moon. This particular arrangement of planets is known as a T-square. It is the worst of all possible astrological aspects. The planets involved in this T-square are interesting, also. The focal point of the T-square is Mars, the planet of war, violence, and aggression.

May 10, 1941, was the date of the worst bombing raid of the war on London. The Germans dropped incendiary bombs, which the winds whipped into a firestorm that destroyed 10,000 buildings and killed thousands of people.

If you look at what was going on in the world on that day, you could almost say it was the low point of civilization for the twentieth century. Stalin was in power in Russia, Tojo in Japan, Hitler had conquered most of Europe, and England was fighting alone against the Germans. And this is reflected in the astrological aspects of that time period.

A few years later, the planets had shifted into a very positive configuration on June 6, 1944, the date of D-Day, the Allied invasion of Europe.

As we can see from a look at the astrological chart on that date, eight of the ten planets are arranged in positive aspect with each other.

The events of that time reflect these positive aspects. The Normandy invasion represented a group of brave men willing to sacrifice themselves to free the continent of Europe from tyranny, and this bravery is shown in the astrological aspects.

Pluto, the planet of will, is conjunct Mars, the planet of action. Pluto and Mars together represent a kind of do-or-die type of energy. I can't think of anything more do-or-die than landing on the Normandy beaches.

Another reflection of these positive astrological aspects was the outcome of the invasion. It was ultimately successful, largely because of its auspicious beginning.

What I have tried to show you here is how past astrological aspects have matched the events that were occurring on the earth at the time. Now for the future.

September 30, 1998

In 1998, the Day of Atonement falls on the 30th of September. A look at the planetary positions on that date shows some remarkable astrological aspects. The sun, the moon, Mercury, Venus, Uranus, Neptune, and Pluto are all lined up in positive aspect. The sun, Mercury, and Venus are together in sign of Libra. They are sextile Pluto, a positive aspect, and trine Uranus, Neptune, and the moon, an even more positive aspect.

The sun is the ego; Mercury, the mind; and Venus is love. These are lined up with Pluto, which is awareness; Uranus, the psychic; and Neptune, the mystic. Who is the most loving, aware, psychic, and mystic person in history? Jesus. In short, these are perfect astrological aspects for the return of Jesus.

Uranus, Neptune, and the moon are together in the sign of Aquarius, and this marks the beginning of the Age of Aquarius, the 1,000 years of peace predicted by the Bible and Cayce.

In Matthew 24 Jesus predicts that prior to the Second Coming there will be a great tribulation, a time of trouble "such as was not since the beginning of the world to this time, no, nor ever shall be" (v. 21). So before September of '98 we would expect to see extremely bad astrological aspects. This is indeed the case.

In August of 1998, Saturn is negatively aspected to the

May 10, 1941

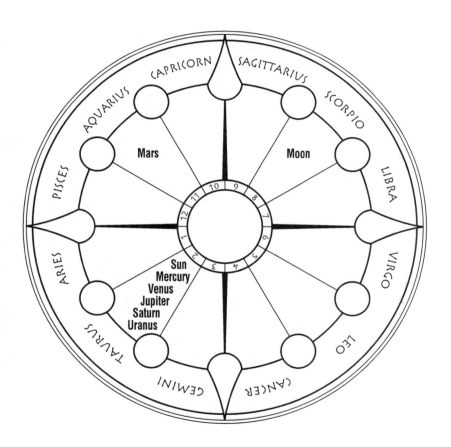

June 6, 1994
D–Day

Uranus-Neptune conjunction in Aquarius. While this is happening, the sun, Venus, and Mars move through the sign of Leo, setting up a T-square aspect with Saturn, Uranus, and Neptune. A T-square is the worst of all possible aspects in astrology. Saturn represents change, and Uranus represents extremes, so August of 1998 will be a period of extreme change. These changes may involve earth changes or war in the Middle East.

Once this T-square is over, the sun, moon, Venus, and Mercury will swing around and line up in the extremely positive position that will be in place on September 30, the Day of Atonement. Or as Cayce calls it, At-one-ment.

If Cayce is correct in saying that Jesus will return in 1998, then I believe that September 30 is the day. But I would not want to get too dogmatic about specific dates because, as they say, if you are too dogmatic, then one day your karma will run over your dogma.

From Pisces to Aquarius

Another important astrological event that is occurring during this time period is that we are currently moving from the Age of Pisces to the Age of Aquarius. Because of the movement of the Earth with respect to the background stars, every 2,165 years we move from one astrological age to the next.

One fascinating thing about this is that every time we change from one astrological age to the next, our religious symbols change also. During the previous age, the Age of Aries, the religious symbols revolved around the sign of Aries, a fire sign that is symbolized by the ram. The religious rituals that were used then involved sacrificing rams on an altar of fire. This took place in the Jewish Temple in Jerusalem and is discussed at length in the Old Testament of the Bible. Other religious fire symbols during that time included the menora, a candlestand in the

August 1998

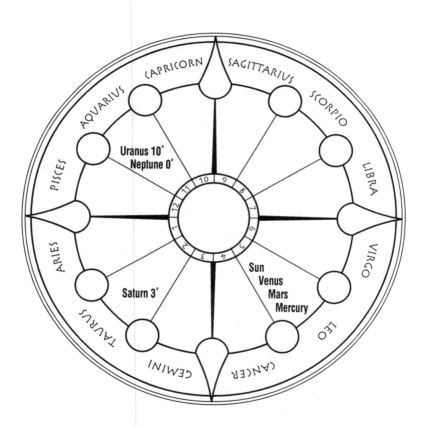

September 30, 1998
Day of Atonement

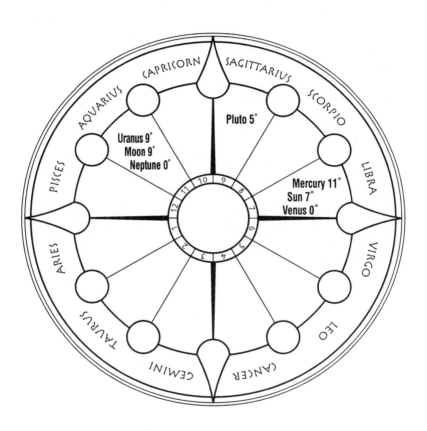

Temple whose candles were kept burning constantly by attending priests.

The Age of Aries ended when the Temple was desecrated by a Syrian king, Antiocus Epiphanes, in 165 B.C.

The present age, the Age of Pisces, has religious symbols that revolve around the sign of Pisces, a water sign symbolized by the fish. Jesus was the physical embodiment of the Piscean Age. He walked on water, calmed the water, was baptized in water, turned water into wine, multiplied the fishes and the loaves, called the fish into the nets, and He was even called the fisher of men. People today even use the Greek word for fish, Icthus, as a symbol for Jesus.

In addition Pisces is the martyr's sign, and the Piscean Age began with the martyrdom of Jesus.

The next age, the Age of Aquarius, will have religious symbols that will revolve around the sign of Aquarius, an air sign symbolized by a man carrying a pitcher of water. This New Age will begin with the 1,000 years of peace predicted in the Bible and by Cayce. It will be characterized by a world united in universal kinship, and it will begin in 1998.

THE REVELATION

The Book of Revelation is a maze of symbols and archetypes that can be interpreted on both literal and symbolic levels. Much of the literal side of Revelation has been covered in our look at Old Testament prophecies, so in this chapter we will deal only with the symbolic interpretation.

"The Revelation" does not refer just to the Book of Revelation but to a revelation that will sweep the entire world at the beginning of the New Age. This new awareness is what the Book of Revelation deals with, and so this will be our starting point. Edgar Cayce gave a series of readings on The Revelation in which he related its symbolism to the human body. It is this understanding of the human body that will be the breakthrough in conventional religious thought that will lead us into the New Age.

This new understanding involves the seven endocrine glands of the body and is symbolized repeatedly in the Book of Revelation:

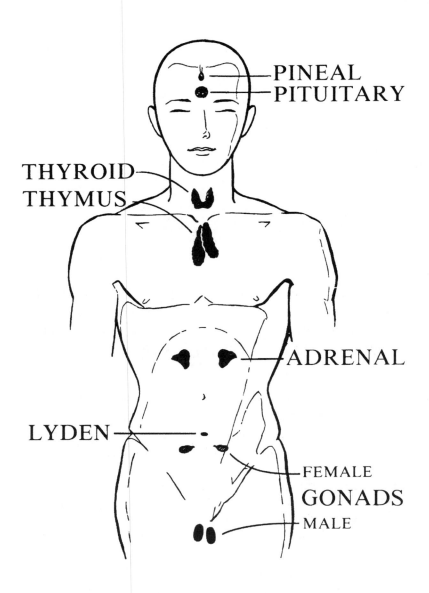

All these "sevens" in Revelation are important to us. The Cayce readings tell us that these "sevens" symbolically represent the seven endocrine centers of the human body.

These endocrine centers are known to the Eastern religions as chakras. They are the pituitary, pineal, thyroid, thymus, adrenals, lyden, and the gonads. During meditation, energy known as kundalini is raised from the lyden and gonads through the nerve centers, up the spine to the brain, and finally to the pineal and pituitary glands. It is this upward flow of energy that allows a person to get in touch with his or her spiritual self. Cayce links these seven glands with the seven churches mentioned in the Book of Revelation and with the colors associated with each of the glands:

1. Pituitary ... Violet – Laodicea – Highest Center
2. Pineal .... Indigo – Philadelphia – Third Eye
3. Thyroid ... Blue/Gray – Sardis – Will
4. Thymus ... Green – Thyatira – Self-Gratification
5. Adrenals ... Yellow – Pergamos – Self-Preservation
6. Lyden ...... Orange – Smyrna – Sustenance
7. Gonads .... Red – Ephesus – Propagation of Species

The existence of these seven glands fits with what is known as the Law of Octaves. In music you move up seven notes before moving to a new octave: do, re, mi, fa, so, la, ti, do. The same is true of the endocrine system. We must move upward through this system in order to move out of what we call our physical universe.

The Law of Octaves is also demonstrated in nature by the fact that the genetic code, which transmits hereditary traits to offspring, contains 64 (8x8) bits of information. We include it in our own systems in the 64 elements of the I Ching, 64 squares on a chess board, and the arrangement of all computers on a base 16 (2x8) system. The Law of Octaves is present in all levels of nature.

Jesus said, "Destroy this temple, and in three days I will raise it up." (John 2:19) He was referring to the temple of the body, which He raised three days after His crucifixion. This is not the only human body symbolism in the Bible. In Revelation the beast rising out of the water symbolically represents the animal influences of the four lower centers: the thymus, adrenals, lyden, and gonads. In a similar vein, the sea of glass in Revelation 4:6 represents the calm emotions of John at the time of his vision. We meet the Father by calming our mind in meditation. This is symbolized by the sea of glass before the throne, the symbol for the brain. To complete the symbolism in chapter 5, the four and twenty elders represent the twenty-four cranial nerves of the brain's five senses.

Running between the seven endocrine centers and all the other centers in the body is the nervous system, referred to in the following section of Ecclesiastes as the "silver cord."

Ecclesiastes 12:5-7:

Also when they shall be afraid of that which is high, and fears shall be in the way, and the almond tree shall flourish, and the grasshopper shall be a burden, and the desire shall fail; because man goes to his long home, and the mourners go about the streets;

Or ever the silver cord is loosed or the golden bowl is broken, or the pitcher is broken at the

fountain, or the wheel broken at the cistern;

Then shall the dust return to the earth as it was, and the spirit shall return to God, who gave it.

These verses are referring to the death of the body after the death of the nervous system. Electrical discharges produce a silver color, and the nervous system has a weak electrical current. So, this section of Ecclesiastes speaks of the human consciousness as contained within the nervous system. No doubt this is true, since everything we see, feel, smell, hear, and taste is associated with the nerves of the body.

These nerves are also closely associated with the seven endocrine centers. The seven glands affect the size of our bodies, our emotional and mental states, and just about everything else we are. Before we go any further, it would be useful for us to examine each of these centers and their effects individually.

1. Gonads. The sexual center is the most basic center of all, since it is involved with the production of our physical bodies. Just as protons and electrons came together in the beginning to form hydrogen, the first element, so male and female come together to form our physical bodies. Thus, this center is linked to the production of matter. As we will see, it is a very important point that the lower centers are linked to matter, and the higher centers are linked to energy.

On the negative side the sex center provides lust, and on the positive side it provides opportunities for souls to enter the earth plane as newborn babies.

2. Lyden. There is not much information on the lyden. Cayce tells us it is involved with sustenance, or the absorption of food matter. It is the point in the passage of energy through the system.

3. Adrenals. The adrenals are the glands of fear. They give us that sudden rush of tension when we are in danger.

For their size the adrenals have a very large blood supply, so that their secretions can get into the bloodstream in a hurry. Meaner and more combative animals have a wide adrenal cortex, while smaller, more timid animals have a narrow adrenal cortex. Humans have the widest adrenal cortex of all. As a lower center, the adrenals produce fear hormones, fear being one of the most destructive emotions of all. It is no coincidence that fear is associated with a lower center, while its opposite, faith, is associated with the higher centers.

4. Thymus. The thymus is called the gland of childhood because it is associated with our development at that stage. It stimulates the production of antibodies that protect the body from disease. The thymus is linked to the muscles and nutrition within our bodies. Cayce says that its emotion is love, and its location in the chest area may have something to do with the "heartache" we feel at times while in love.

5. Thyroid. The Cayce readings tell us that the thyroid is the gland of the will. This fits with what medical science tells us, since the thyroid controls the amount of energy used in the body. Its hormone, thyroxin, controls energy output. If a person applies his or her will, he or she can always find enough energy to accomplish a task. The thyroid is the pivotal point between the four lower centers and the two higher ones. The will controls which way the consciousness will go.

6. Pineal. René Descartes in his book, *Trait de L' Homme* in 1662, located the human soul in the pineal gland. Two thousand years ago the Hindus said the pineal was the "seat of the soul." Today, the pineal is often called the "third eye." This is fascinating, since the cells in the pineal are almost identical to the cells in the retina of the eye. This may be why flashes of light are seen in higher states of consciousness. The mystical symbolism of the pineal is seen in the eye encased in the pyramid on the U.S. dollar bill. The pineal usually atrophies at age seven, which may be why Jesus said if we do not become "as little children," we cannot enter the kingdom of heaven. The pineal is the gateway to the highest center of all, the pituitary, since the pineal sits on the bundled nerves of the thalamus from which the pituitary hangs.

7. Pituitary. The pituitary is called the master gland by scientists because it controls all the other glands. It is about the size of an almond dangling from the end of a group of nerves known as the hypothalamus. The pituitary is so important to the body that removal will cause death in three days. It has its own skull, known as the turkish saddle, which cradles it within our larger skull. Sexual development is one of the pituitary's functions, along with its more famous function of controlling the growth of the body. Underaction of the pituitary produces dwarfs; overaction produces giants.

Recent studies have shown that the pituitary produces natural painkillers known as endorphins. Western scientists have found that yogis trained in meditation can endure great physical pain by their production of endorphins. These endorphins may also be the cause of the "bliss" many people experience in meditation.

Last, but not least, the pituitary controls the salt content of the body. The salt content of any liquid is directly related to its electrical conductivity. It is possible that this would explain why healers, such as Jesus, could produce power to heal. Certainly, this power also comes from higher levels, but at some point it must manifest itself on this level. Electrical impulses may be one of these manifestations.

These are only a few of the capabilities of the pituitary. Dozens of hormones that it produces have been isolated, many of which are unknown in their function. Ultimately, we will discover that the pituitary is unlimited in its functions. In meditation it is the point at which we enter the holy of holies within ourselves.

In light of our study of the two higher glands it is important at this point to examine the involvement of the brain during meditation. The human brain has been compared to a "delicate flower perched on the end of a slender stalk." There are three sections in the brain called units. The third unit is concerned with planning and movement of the body. The second unit is concerned with the analysis of sensory input, e.g., seeing, hearing, etc. The first unit is the power supply. It is this unit that concerns us.

The *Encyclopedia of the Human Body* describes the first unit as follows:

> **"The first functional unit is located at the base of the brain and consists of the reticular formation, the midbrain, the thalamus, and the hypothalamus. It is the first area encountered by inputs from the sense organs and information stemming from the metabolic functions within the body. This unit plays a role in the regulation of activity in the cortex and maintains the alertness of the higher areas of the brain. It does this not by single isolated nerve impulses but by waves of electrical activity spreading throughout the unit and traveling up to the cortex. It is similar to a power source, which feeds the higher areas and which, if removed, causes a state of drowsiness."**

The pituitary and pineal are connected to the first unit at the hypothalamus and thalamus. During meditation the third unit of the brain is "shut off" by sitting still and not moving the body. The second unit is likewise shut off by clearing the mind of conscious thought. The only thing left is the first unit. As the quote indicates, waves of electrical energy flow up the spine to the thalamus, pineal, and the pituitary. This is the kundalini energy mentioned earlier. It is interesting to note that proper meditation requires calm emotions, and the thalamus, when diseased, produces fits of strong emotion. So the flow of energy in the thalamus is linked to the emotions, the sea of glass, mentioned in The Revelation by John.

All of this has been preached by mystics for thousands of years and is what Jesus meant when He said, "The kingdom of God is within you."

The Cayce readings have a great deal to say about the kundalini, as seen in the following readings:

Q. Are the following statements true or false? Comment on each as I read it: The life force rises directly from the Leydig gland through the Gonads, thence to Pineal, and then to the other centers.

A. This is correct; though, to be sure, as it rises and is distributed through the other centers it returns to the solar plexus area for its impulse through the system.

For the moment, let's consider the variation here in this life force – or as respecting this life force. The question is asked not in relation to the life alone as manifested in the human body, but as to the process through which coordination is attained or gained in and through meditation, see?

Hence, physically, as we have indicated, there is first the nucleus – or the union of the first activities; and then the pineal as the long thread activity to the center of the brain, see? Then from there, as development progresses, there are those activities through reflexes to the growth or the developing of the body.

Interpret that variation, then, as being indicated here. One life force is the body-growth, as just described. The other is the impulse that arises, from the life center, in meditation. (281-53)

Q. How can I overcome the nerve strain I'm under at times?

A. By closing the eyes and meditating from within, so that there arises – through that of the nerve system – that necessary element that makes along the PINEAL (Don't forget that this runs from the toes to the crown of the head!), that will quiet the whole nerve forces, making for that – as has been given – as the TRUE bread, the true strength of life itself. Quiet, meditation, for a half to a minute, will bring strength – [if the body will] see PHYSICALLY this flowing out to quiet self, whether walking, standing still, or resting. Well, too, that OFT, when alone MEDITATE in the silence – as the body HAS done.   (311-4)

These readings show us that the flow of energy involves not only meditation, but body growth as well. This agrees with what medical science has told us. This flow of energy must be directed to spiritual things or it can be harmful. If used in the spirit of love and for the good of all, it can become a great light as the following reading shows:

In the body we find that which connects the pineal, the pituitary, the lyden, may be truly called the silver cord, or the golden cup that may be filled with a closer walk with that which is the creative essence in physical, mental and spiritual life; for the destruction wholly of either will make for the disintegration of the soul from its house of clay. To be purely material minded, were an anatomical or pathological study made for a period of seven years (which is a cycle of change in all the body-elements) of one that is acted upon through the third eye alone, we will find one fed upon spiritual things becomes a light that may shine from and in the darkest corner. One fed upon the purely

**material will become a Frankenstein that is without
a concept of any influence other than material or
mental.**   **(262-20)**

In this reading Cayce mentions the "silver cord," as
written about in Ecclesiastes, which may be "filled with a
closer walk with . . . the creative essence" (God). It is
interesting to note that Cayce says that one who acts
through the third eye alone for seven years (the period it
takes for every cell in the body to replace itself) would
become a light to the world, while one fed only on the
material world would become a Frankenstein monster! It
is easy to think of examples of materially minded people in
the world. But it is encouraging to note that all of us can
develop spiritually in just seven years if we so desire.

Development through meditation involves not only the
act of meditation itself but meditation with the highest
possible purpose – in other words, being a channel of
God's gifts to one's fellow human. What are these gifts?
Love, patience, long-suffering, and forgiveness, to name
just a few. With these purposes in mind meditation can
become a most sublime and joyous experience.

I have been meditating for a number of years, so my
experiences with meditation have been many and varied.
Many times I have received guidance from the "still, small
voice within." Usually, this guidance has been of great help
to me. The only bad experience I can remember involved
an insect that insisted on buzzing around my ear during
my meditation. This buzzing was such a disturbance that
the end of the meditation period found me exhausted from
attempting to concentrate in an agitated frame of mind.
The mind must be calm to properly meditate.

The rising of kundalini energy in meditation can be
experienced in a variety of ways. It can be seen as a series
of waves spreading outward from a single point, then
dissipating and starting over again. It spreads like ripples in

a pond when you toss in a rock. Or, to put it another way, it looks like water poured on flat concrete which spreads out in a circle from a single point. It slowly flows into one's consciousness.

Another kundalini experience is the bright light or, as some call it, "seeing the light." It comes as a light brighter than any light ever seen with the eyes, except that it is in the mind's eye. Once, when I was falling asleep, I was viewing an extremely bright sunset. I was in a meditative state inside a totally dark room. I reacted to the sunset by trying to close my eyes but found they were already closed! I have experienced this "light" several times since then, and it always occurs as an incredibly bright light between the eyes, the exact location of the pineal, the third eye.

The most vivid kundalini energy I have ever experienced happened to me in a recent meditation session. I had been reading about raising energy up the spine and was attempting to do so just to see how much I could raise. This is not a good idea, because your purposes must be more pure than just having an "experience." As I was raising this energy, I visualized in my mind someone turning off a light. At the instant the light was turned off, I heard a loud audible snap! It sounded like a crackle of electricity or the snap of a bullwhip. At the same time I felt the energy flow that was going up my spine shut off with a sudden jolt. It was an unsettling experience that taught me that kundalini is not something to be toyed with.

As the Cayce readings have said, this electrical energy is not just for the growth of the body. The readings go even further:

Thus there are the vibrations of the electrical energies of the body, for Life itself is electrical. . .
(281-27)

About fifty years ago, a Yale University neuroanatomist named Harold Burr found that there are electrical currents within all living organisms, from seeds to human beings. He theorized that this electromagnetic field doesn't just reflect the electrical activity of the cells it envelops; it also controls and organizes them. Burr described it as "nature's jello mold," shaping living matter just as a magnetic field patterns iron filings.

Magnifying all this is the fact that the brain is the most electrical organ in the body. Neurons account for only twenty percent of the brain's cells; the rest are mostly glial cells that sheathe the neurons. Evidence has been found that a direct current flows steadily through the glial cells. Some scientists now believe that this direct current system, generally ignored by most brain researchers, may be the body's natural mechanism for cellular growth and repair. Science is gradually catching up with what the readings revealed many years ago.

This electrical current is very important to the theories we will look at next. The higher centers of the body are centers of energy, and the lower centers are more closely associated with matter.

The importance of this can be understood when one has a grasp of Einstein's theory of relativity: As an object approaches the speed of light, time slows down. When said object reaches the speed of light, time stops. In other words, at the speed of light time does not move. This part of Einstein's theory was proven in 1936 by Bell Laboratories. A radiating atom can act as a clock because it emits light at a definite frequency and wavelength in precise intervals. This can be measured by a spectroscope. Bell Labs compared the light given off by hydrogen atoms at high velocities with that of hydrogen atoms at rest. It was discovered that the frequency of vibration of the fast-moving atoms slowed down in the exact manner Einstein had predicted. Another way of putting it would be that as the atoms speeded up, time slowed down.

Another example involves space travel. If a man left earth in a spaceship traveling at the speed of light, when he reached his destination he would be the same age as when he left. Even if several years had passed for people on the earth, our space traveler would not have aged at all. Even at the slow speeds automobiles and airplanes travel, time slows down, however slight the change may be. The change only becomes noticeable when speeds approach the speed of light, an incredible 186,000 miles per second.

All energy moves about the universe at the speed of light. So to energy and light, time is totally meaningless. Einstein put it as follows: "For us believing physicists time has the value of mere illusion, however tenacious." So time is an illusion belonging to the world of matter and not to the world of energy.

We know that consciousness operates through energy because the only thing that separates a dead body from a living body is electrical energy. The body without electricity is dead matter. At that point it exists only at the vibratory level of matter and not at the level from which our consciousness flows, which is energy.

The train of logic is as follows: The direct current flow of electricity in the human brain moves at 99.999% of the speed of light in the wake of our consciousness. Our consciousness exists at the level from which light and energy come, where time is stopped. If our consciousness exists where time is standing still, then our consciousness is eternal. Our brain acts as a brake to slow our consciousness down enough that it can operate at a level where the illusion of time does exist in our physical universe. This is the scientific proof that life is eternal. This is why the higher centers of the body are associated with energy, and the lower centers of the body are associated with matter.

If you raise your consciousness in meditation, you connect with the energy level and your Eternal Being.

Until recently, this ramification of the theory of relativity was ignored, but now many people are beginning to look at the relationship between time, consciousness, and energy. Several books have been written on this subject, and in the latter quarter of the twentieth century, discoveries in the world of physics will help awaken the world to the existence of eternal life.

The raising of consciousness to connect with the "eternal now" is the subject of the following Cayce reading:

As this life-force is expanded, it moves first from the Leydig center through the adrenals, in what may be termed an upward trend, to the pineal and to the centers in control of the emotions – or reflexes through the nerve forces of the body.

Thus an entity puts itself, through such an activity, into association or in conjunction with all it has EVER been or may be. For, it loosens the physical consciousness to the universal conscious-ness.   (2475-1)

Notice that Cayce says that moving upward to the pineal puts a person in contact with the past, present, and the future, the place where time does not move and all time is one. This is the universal consciousness or God. Through this raising of energy we connect with God. This is nothing new. Mystics have been saying this for thousands of years, but now we know more about it through the realm of physics.

There are, of course, many connections between God and light energy. The sun, the source of all life and light, is the most obvious connection. Jesus emitted a light or aura which Matthew says was as "white as snow." Eastern mystics talk about achieving "enlightenment," with the middle syllable being the word "light."

The Bible is full of references to light. Some are

references to spiritual light, but there is more in their meaning. Paul saw a great light on the road to Damascus that changed him from persecuting the Christians to joining them. Here are just a few biblical references to light:

I John 1:5 "This then is the message which we have heard of him and declare to you, that God is light."

John 8:12 "I am the light of the world; he that follows me shall not walk in darkness, but shall have the light of life."

John 12:36 "While you have light, believe in the light, that you may be the Sons of Light."

Matthew 6:22 "The light of the body is the eye."

Light is often used as a symbol of spirituality, even to the point of saying, "God is Light." Jesus referred to Himself as the "light of the world" and to the light of the body as the "eye" or the third eye. Thus, Jesus has shown that the energy flow to the third eye is the spiritual light of the human body. This is the most important point in these references, because it shows the way of development for all of us.

In one of his readings. Cayce described the use of light appearing in a six-sided crystal as a "means of communication between infinitity and the finite." (2072-10) Since the source of light itself is the infinite, it would make sense that one could communicate with the "infinite" in this way. Just what this communication would mean we can only guess at this stage of our development.

One of the Cayce readings we looked at earlier referred to Jesus returning and receiving as many as had "quickened" themselves through living a spiritual life. All of the universe, matter and energy, is made up of vibrations. Energy is a quicker vibration than matter. The use of meditation and spiritual living quickens the body of matter to the level of energy, and beyond to the universal consciousness. "Quickening" is a perfect description of an increase in the frequency of vibrations, that is, a shift from matter to energy.

The raising of consciousness is central to the Second Coming: first, because the raising of vibrations among the human race is what will attract Jesus to return; second, because if one gets in touch with his or her eternal spirit, then physical death has no power. If earth changes occur, many people will die. But if they have quickened themselves, their spirits will live on and reincarnate during the millennium. So those who quicken themselves will survive, even if they die.

Many books about the Second Coming speak of survival in terms of storing food and such, but true survival is based on the growth of a person's soul. This is the message of Jesus' death and resurrection.

The idea of light and the raising of consciousness is relevant to the Second Coming for a number of other reasons. It represents the change that will occur in religious thought throughout the world. People will develop themselves through meditation, and science will come to recognize this development. Particularly, the science of physics will lead the way in the field of understanding consciousness.

This understanding of consciousness includes much more than just the consciousness of humanity. Physics is moving toward understanding the universe and universal consciousness, an idea that has been held by Eastern religions for many years. The universe has been described as a thought in the mind of God, and now physicists are saying that the universe behaves more like "a great thought than a machine."

One of the most important theories developed in physics in the last few years is called Bell's theorem. In a series of very complicated mathematical proofs, physicist J.S. Bell has shown that everything in the universe is connected to everything else, even though they may be separated by great distances. In other words, everything is part of one thing, i.e., God, the Creative Force, etc.

There is evidence for this in other scientific truths. German physicist Max Planck proved that all energy radiations were a function of one number, now known as "Planck's constant." If all energy is a function of one number, then surely all energy is a function of one thing. This one thing is the Creative Force or God.

Einstein proved that energy and matter were essentially equivalent, or were different vibratory levels of the same thing. Energy and matter are part of one force, or, as the Bible says, "The Lord thy God is One."

This can be shown mathematically with Einstein's famous equivalence equation:

$$E=mc^2$$

divide both sides by E

$$\frac{E}{E} = \frac{mc^2}{E} \qquad 1 = \frac{mc^2}{E}$$

The information we have just looked at proves that the universe is a part of one whole. This whole is both physical and nonphysical. Physical things exist in the third dimension, but the universe was created from the fourth dimension, the dimension of consciousness. Time is not the fourth dimension as many believe; thought, ideas, and consciousness are the fourth dimension. Before anything exists in the physical universe, it must first be an idea. Before a bridge is built, someone must think of the idea of building it. The same is true of the creation of the universe. God conceived of the universe first, and it was created. The point here is that the three-dimensional One we are part of is only part of the universal consciousness. Three-dimensional reality is only a shadow of the spiritual reality. Everything in reality follows the same pattern: fourth-dimensional idea – creative action – third-dimensional reality. This is the way our three-dimensional universe was created and is still being created today.

THE HALL OF RECORDS

According to the Cayce readings, during the last part of this century, probably coinciding with the Second Coming, humankind will make the greatest archaeological discovery of all time. This discovery will involve the Egyptian pyramids at Gizeh. The Great Pyramid and the Sphinx will yield treasures beyond the wildest dream of any Egyptologist.

The story of Gizeh goes back many thousands of years, before the Great Flood of Noah's time. During those ancient times, according to the readings, a king by the name of Arart moved his tribe into the Nile Valley and conquered the natives there. Arart's spiritual leader was a priest by the name of Ra Ta (a previous incarnation of Edgar Cayce). Inspired from on high, Ra Ta conceived a spiritual monument to last for all time, what is now known as the Great Pyramid at Gizeh. Hermes, who is often mentioned in Egyptian legends, was the architect of the project:

. . .the entering in of Hermes WITH Ra – who came as one of the peoples from the mount to

which these peoples had been banished. . . Hence
under the authority of Ra, and Hermes as the guide,
or the actual (as would be termed in the present)
constructing or construction architect with the
priest or Ra giving the directions. . .   (294-151)

Arart's son, Araaraart, was king at the time of the
completion of the project which, is much older than
generally believed.

> Q. *What was the date of the actual beginning and
> ending of the construction of the Great Pyramid?*
> A. Was one hundred years in construction. Be-
> gun and completed in the period of Araaraart's
> time, with Hermes and Ra.

> Q. *What was the date B.C. of that period?*
> A. 10,490 to 10,390 before the Prince entered
> into Egypt.   (5748-6)

The Great Pyramid was built by the use of forces we are
only now beginning to rediscover.

> Q. *How was this particular Great Pyramid of
> Gizeh built?*
> A. By the use of those forces in nature as make
> for iron to swim. Stone floats in the air in the same
> manner. This will be discovered in '58.   (5748-6)

> Q. *By what power or powers were these early
> pyramids and temples constructed?*
> A. By the lifting forces of those gases that are
> being used gradually in the present civilization,
> and by the fine work or activities of those versed
> in that pertaining to the source from which all
> power comes.   (5750-1)

The force in nature that causes "iron to swim" is
buoyancy. Buoyancy has been known since the time of

Archimedes, but the method for focusing this force was not known until 1958 and still isn't totally understood. Many important discoveries were made in 1958 including the invention of the laser. Since the readings say that the Atlanteans aided in the construction of the Pyramid, and since the readings also say that the principal source of power for the Atlantean civilization was light focused on a crystal, the laser may have been the method by which the forces of buoyancy were controlled.

For there was not only the adding to the monuments, but the Atlanteans aided in their activities with the creating of that called the Pyramid, with its records of events of the earth through its activity in all ages to that in which the new dispensation is to come.   (281-43)

The Great Pyramid was constructed in a manner such that it would be difficult, if not impossible, to reproduce it today. It contains 2,300,000 stones, many weighing as much as 20 tons. Its blocks are fitted together so finely that a razor blade cannot fit between the blocks of the Great Pyramid. The technology used in its construction is superior to ours today because it was built by Atlanteans.

According to the readings, the continent of Atlantis existed for thousands of years at a state of technology far beyond today's. But because of the misuse of this technology, the continent began to break up and sink into what is now the Atlantic Ocean. The total destruction took place over many years, and some Atlanteans escaped and found their way to Egypt and the Nile Valley.

Many Egyptologists would say that this story is pure fantasy, but several facts dispute this. The large pyramids in Egypt were allegedly tombs for ancient pharaohs, yet no bodies have ever been found in any of the larger pyramids. Grave robbers are always cited as the reason for this, but to reach the King's Chamber of the Great Pyramid, explorers had to dig around a 29-foot granite plug. When they reached the King's Chamber, it was empty. If grave robbers had been there before the exploration, would they have plugged the passage with a 29-foot-thick granite stone to protect an empty tomb?

The priest Ra and Hermes incorporated mathematics into the Pyramid, including the relationship of pi and phi. This clearly shows that their knowledge of science was greater than that believed to be possessed by ancient humanity. These mathematical relations were not supposed to have been discovered until much later.

Geographical considerations also went into the building of the Great Pyramid:

> **When the lines about the earth are considered from the mathematical precisions, it will be found that the center is nigh unto where the Great Pyramid, which was begun then, is still located.**
> **(281-42)**

> **At the correct time accurate imaginary lines can be drawn from the opening of the great Pyramid to the second star in the Great Dipper, called Polaris or the North Star. This indicates it is the system toward which the soul takes its flight after having completed its sojourn through this solar system.**
> **(5748-6)**

The Great Pyramid is arranged in a perfect north-south alignment, so close that after thousands of years it is off axis by only an inch or so. The entrance to the inner chambers is on an angle that faces directly toward Polaris. This indicates that each soul goes to that system after completing the cycle in this solar system. This is one of the more esoteric messages built into the Great Pyramid.

Much has been written in recent years of the special properties of the pyramid shape itself. Books about "pyramid power" have testified to the ability of pyramids to do everything from sharpening razor blades to mummifying fruit. These effects are caused by the ability of the pyramid to focus cosmic energy. A pyramid can do this because it is a model of three-dimensional reality. If you take a two-dimensional square and use only one point to make it a three-dimensional object, the result is a pyramid. The Great Pyramid focuses cosmic energy by mirroring three-dimensional reality in on itself, in the same way that opposing mirrors make smaller and smaller images of each other into infinity.

The ability to focus energy is even contained in the name, "pyramid." "Pyra" comes from the word for fire, "pyro"; and "mid" means middle. So "pyramid" means "fire in the middle" or a focus of cosmic energy.

The Great Pyramid is built largely of limestone blocks that are made of small crystals. Limestone crystals are known for their even vibration and were chosen in order to focus the Pyramid's vibrations evenly. More will undoubtedly be learned about pyramid energy in the future as it is studied by modern-day science.

Not only is the Great Pyramid a focus of energy but it incorporates in its stones and inner passages the history and future of humanity:

> . . .the rise and fall of the nations were to be depicted in this same temple that was to act as an interpreter for that which had been, that which is, and that which is to be, in the material plane.
>
> (294-151)

> This, then, receives all the records from the beginnings of that given by the priest, Arart, Araaraart and Ra, to that period when there is to be the change in the earth's position and the return of the Great Initiate to that and other lands for the folding up of those prophecies that are depicted

> there. All changes that came in the religious thought
> in the world are shown there, in the variations in
> which the passage through same is reached, from
> the base to the top – or to the open tomb AND the
> top. These are signified by both the layer and the
> color in what direction the turn is made.   (5748-5)

The rise and fall of nations are depicted in the Great
Pyramid along with the changes in religious thought
which will come about in the world. This can be seen by
examining the passages. The first passage is descending,
and this undoubtedly represents the fall of humankind
from grace. The next passage is ascending, which represents our ascent from the birth of Jesus to the present age.
The stone prophecies continue until the return of the
Great Initiate, Jesus, at the end of this age, 1998.

During Jesus' studies in Egypt, the Great Pyramid was
used as a Hall of Initiation for Him and John the Baptist
into the knowledge of One God.

> Then, with Hermes and Ra (those that assumed
> or took up the work of Araaraart) there began the
> building of that now called Gizeh, with which those
> prophecies that had been in the Temple of Records
> and the Temple Beautiful were builded, in the
> building of this that was to be the hall of the
> initiates of that sometimes referred to as the White
> Brotherhood.   (5748-5)

> In this same pyramid did the Great Initiate, the
> Master, take those last of the Brotherhood degrees
> with John, the forerunner of Him, at that place.
>   (5748-5)

This initiation involved breaking the cycle of death and
rebirth, which Jesus did so dramatically with His resurrection.
The initiation in the Great Pyramid was a symbolic prelude
to this.

Q. Please describe Jesus' initiation in Egypt, telling if the Gospel reference to "three days and nights in the grave or tomb," possibly in the shape of a cross, indicate a special initiation.

A. This is a portion of the initiation – it is a part of the passage through that to which each soul is to attain in its development, as has the world through each period of their incarnation in the earth. As is supposed, the record of the earth through the passage through the tomb, or the pyramid, is that through which each entity, each soul, as an initiate must pass for the attaining to the releasing of same – as indicated by the empty tomb, which has NEVER been filled, see? Only Jesus was able to break same, as it became that which indicated His fulfillment.   (2067-70)

Each soul in the earth plane must pass through the same sort of initiation in order to break the death cycle. Part of this initiation will be the darkness that will overcome the sun before the Second Coming. A more important part will be the recognition by everyone that death is not the end of life.

Of the prophecies represented in the Great Pyramid Cayce mentions several specifically:

Q. Are the deductions and conclusions arrived at by D. Davidson and H. Aldersmith in their book on The Great Pyramid correct?

A. Many of these that have been taken as deductions are correct. Many are far overdrawn. Only an initiate may understand.

Q. What corrections for the period of the 20th century?

A. Only those that there will be an upheaval in '36.

*Q. Do you mean there will be an upheaval in '36
as recorded in the pyramid?*

A. As recorded in the pyramid, though this is
set for a correction, which, as has been given, is
between '32 AND '38 – the correction would be,
for this – as seen – is '36 – for it is in many – these
run from specific days; for, as has been seen,
there are periods when even the hour, day, year,
place, country, nation, town, and individuals are
pointed out. That's how correct are many of
those prophecies as made.   (5748-5)

According to Cayce, some of the prophecies in the
Great Pyramid are correct down to the town, day, and
individuals involved. What those prophecies could be, one
can only guess, but no doubt the birth of Jesus is one of the
specific prophecies. Also, there is mentioned an upheaval
in 1936, estimated by the Pyramid's prophecy in stone as
occurring between 1932 and 1938. This upheaval is
explained in the following readings:

A great deal in various experiences of same;
that is, in the interpreting of periods of those activities which preceded that period in which the
building was begun there. For, remember, this
was not an interpretation only from that period
FORWARD, but as to the very PLACE and experience in which there is to be the change in the
activities in the earth!   (849-45)

*Q. What are the correct interpretations of the in-
dications in the Great Pyramid regarding the time
when the present depression will end?*

A. The changes as indicated and outlined are
for the latter part of the present year (1932). As
far as depression is concerned, this is not – as in
the minds of many – because fear has arisen, but

rather that, when fear has arisen in the hearts of the created, sin lieth at the door. Then, the change will occur – or that seeking will make the definite change – in the latter portion of the present year. Not that times financially will be better but the minds of the people will be fitted to the conditions better.

Q. What will be the type and extent of the upheaval in '36?

A. The wars, the upheavals in the interior of the earth, and the shifting of same by the differentiation in the axis as respecting the positions from the Polaris center.   (5748-6)

Two types of upheavals are discussed in this reading: wars and changes in the interior of the earth that will cause the poles to shift. The year 1936 was a turning point for World War II, since it was the year that Hitler became aggressive and marched into the Rhineland. At that time German armed forces were still weak, and if the Allies had resisted, Hitler's dominance of Europe might have been prevented. Also, 1936 was the beginning of the Spanish Civil War, which became a miniversion of the larger war to come, with Fascism fighting democracy.

The upheaval within the earth that occurred in 1936 was apparently at the earth's core and will take time to work its way out. This is understandable since the earth is a revolving mass of molten nickel and iron, whose only solid portion is the thin layer of crust we live on. When a spinning top develops a slight wobble, it takes time to topple over, and the earth is no exception. A slight shift in equilibrium can gradually become a larger one.

Somehow the pole shift is represented in the stones of the Great Pyramid, and the following reading seems to imply that the constellation of Libra is involved.

[The Great Pyramid] was to be the presentation of that which had been gained by these peoples through the activities of Ra Ta, who NOW was known as Ra. . . [and] there was brought the idea of the preservation of these, not only for those in the present but for the generations that were to come in the experiences and experiences throughout that period, until the changes were to come again in the earth's position. . . It was formed according to that which had been worked out by Ra Ta in the mount as related to the position of the various stars, that acted in the place about which this particular solar system circles in its activity, going towards what? That same name as to which the priest was banished – the constellation of Libra, or to Libya were these peoples sent.   (294-151)

It may be that the poles will shift toward Libra, or it may be that the whole solar system will shift. The reading is not clear. Cayce may have been referring to the earth and the moon as a "system." One thing that is known is that all the stars in the galaxy are constantly shifting position, and our sun and the pole star, Polaris, are no exceptions. Neither are the Earth and the moon.

Of all the prophecies depicted in the Great Pyramid the most important has to do with the so-called King's Chamber at the top of the interior passageways. In the King's Chamber is an empty sarcophagus or coffin.

Q. What definite details are indicated as to what will happen after we enter the period of the King's Chamber?

A. When the bridegroom is at hand, all do rejoice. When we enter that understanding of being in the King's presence, with that of the mental seeking, the joy, the buoyancy, the new understanding, the new life, through the period.

The seven stones above the King's Chamber.

Q. What is the significance of the empty sarcophagus?

A. That there will be no more death. Don't misunderstand or misinterpret! But the INTERPRETATION of death will be made plain.

Q. What is the date, as recorded by the Pyramid, of entering in the King's Chamber?

A. '38 to '58.   (5748-6)

The entity saw what was preserved as the memorials, the pyramids built during the entity's sojourn; when there was begun the pyramid of understanding or Gizeh – and only to the king's chamber was the pathway built. But the entity will see in the present the empty tomb period pass; hence rise to heights of activity in the present experience.   (275-33)

The meaning of the empty sarcophagus is that the death of the physical body does not mean the death of the soul. The prophecy connected with this is the return of the bridegroom, Jesus (as He is symbolized in the Bible), and the realization by the whole human race that the spirit survives death. This was the purpose of Jesus' resurrection, to allow a way for us to overcome death and to show that death could be overcome.

Above the empty sarcophagus in the King's Chamber are seven stones. These stones are arranged in the fashion of an arrow, with five stones as the shaft and two stones as the tip. This symbolizes the raising of energy through the seven endocrine centers. When you enter the King's Chamber you say, "Where has the body gone?" It has ascended upward through the seven centers out of the physical plane. Remember that Cayce said that the King's Chamber represented the "changes that came in the religious thought in the world." (5748-5) The most important change in religious thought will be the realization that the seven endocrine centers are the key to spiritual development. And the arrow points the way upward.

The five lower stones in the arrow are made of red granite and represent the five lower centers of the body (thus the color red is used). The two stones at the top are made of gray limestone and represent the pineal and pituitary glands, which are gray. The top two stones are connected, as the pituitary and pineal are connected by the thalamus and the hypothalamus. Even more esoteric is the fact that limestone was used. Lime accumulates in the brain such that years ago physicians called lime salts "brain sand." Also, the pituitary and pineal regulate the amount of lime in the body, so limestone was a perfect symbol for the two higher glands.

On the back of every U.S. dollar bill is a pyramid with an eye in the middle of it. The "eye in the pyramid" symbolizes the pineal or third eye of the body in beautifully mystical fashion. This eye also represents the seven stones above the empty sarcophagus, making one of the United States' most common symbols a very esoteric one.

Next to the Great Pyramid of Gizeh is a monument the readings often call the mystery of mysteries, the Sphinx. Until recent times the Sphinx has been covered with sand up to its neck, but as the time draws near for the Sphinx to reveal its secrets, the whole body of the Sphinx has been uncovered. Its animal body represents humanity's animal nature, and the four lower centers of the body. The head of the Sphinx shows that the human body is not just animalistic but contains a spirit that can overcome its animal nature by developing the two higher centers contained in the head. The Sphinx symbolizes our quest for spiritual development.

It is more than just a symbol, however, because for thousands of years the Sphinx has been guarding a storehouse of historical records known as the Hall of Records. This Hall of Records, buried beneath the sands of Gizeh, contains the history of humankind from the beginning, including the rise and fall of Atlantis.

The entity aided in those activities, being among the children of the Law of One from Atlantis; AIDING the Priest in that preparation, in that manner of building the temples of records that lie just beyond that enigma that still is the mystery of mysteries to those who seek to know what were the manners of thought of the ancient sons who made man – a beast – as a part of the consciousness.
(2402-2)

In the information as respecting the pyramids, their purpose in the experience of the peoples, in the period when there was the rebuilding of the priest during the return in the land, some 10,500 before the coming of the Christ into the land, there was first that attempt to restore and add to that which had been begun on what is called the Sphinx, and the treasure or storehouse facing same, between this and the Nile, in which those records were kept by Arart and Araaraart in the period.   **(5748-5)**

These records, when they are found, will constitute the most incredible archaeological find of all time. They contain not only the history of Atlantis but all of its spiritual truths that have been lost to us for thousands of years.

Q. *In which pyramid or temple are the records mentioned in the readings given through this channel on Atlantis, in April, 1932 [(364) series]?*
A. As given, that temple was destroyed at the time there was the last destruction of Atlantis. Yet, as time draws nigh when changes are to come about, there may be the opening of those three

places where the records are one, to those that are the initiates in the knowledge of the One God:

The temple by Iltar will then rise again. Also there will be the opening of the temple or hall of records in Egypt, and those records that were put into the heart of the Atlantean land may also be found there – that have been kept for those that are of that group. The RECORDS are ONE. (5750-1)

. . .these were to be kept as had been given by the priests in Atlantis or Poseidia (Temple), when these records of the race of the developments, of the laws pertaining to One were put in their chambers. . .
(378-16)

The laws of One are the laws having to do with One God and were given by the priests in Atlantis to be preserved in the Hall of Records. However, there are two other places where the records are also preserved – in the temple of Iltar near the Yucatan in Mexico and underwater off the coast of what is now Bimini. These two locations were given in another reading. In those three places "the RECORDS are ONE."

The records are not in any language with which we are familiar but are written in a combination of Egyptian and Atlantean letters.

The entity was a priestess in the Law of One, and among those who – ill – came into the Egyptian land – as the elders in those groups for preserving the records, as well as for preserving a portion of that race, that peoples.

With the periods of reconstruction after the return of the Priest, the entity joined with those who were active in putting the records in forms that were partially of the old characters of the ancient or early Egyptian, part in the newer form of the Atlanteans. These may be found, especially when the house or tomb of records is opened, in a few years from now.   (2537-1)

Q. Give in detail what the sealed room contains.

A. A record of Atlantis from the beginning of those periods when the Spirit took form or began the encasements in that land, and the developments of the peoples throughout their sojourn, with the records of the first destruction and the changes that took place in the land, with the record of the SOJOURNINGS of the peoples to the varied activities in other lands, and a record of the meetings of all the nations or lands for the activities in the destructions that became necessary with the final destruction of Atlantis and the buildings of the pyramid of initiation, with who, what, where, would come the opening of the records that are as copies from the sunken Atlantis; for with the change it must rise (the temple) again.

This in position lies, as the sun rises from the waters, the line of the shadow (or light) falls between the paws of the Sphinx, that was later set as the sentinel or guard, and which may not be entered from the connecting chambers from the Sphinx's paw (right paw) until the TIME has been fulfilled when the changes must be active in this sphere of man's experience.

Between, then, the Sphinx and the river.

(378-16)

According to Cayce, the records also contain a prophecy of who will find them, when this will happen, and where they will be found. The connecting chambers will be opened from the Sphinx's right paw, and this gives us a tremendous clue as to where the entrance to the Hall

The Sphinx's right front forepaw "box."

Photo by Uwe E. Wilken

of Records is. Of course, people familiar with the readings have examined the Sphinx's right paw for years, and the entrance has not yet been found, but there may be a helpful clue in the following reading.

Q. In what capacity did this entity act regarding the building of the sphinx?

A. As the monuments were being rebuilt in the plains of that now called the pyramid of Gizeh, this entity builded, laid, the foundations; that is, superintended same, figured out the geometrical position of same in relation to those buildings as were put up of that connecting the sphinx. And the data concerning same may be found in the vaults in the base of the sphinx. We see this sphinx was builded as this:

The excavations were made for same in the plains above where the temple of Isis had stood during the deluge, occurring some centuries before, when this people (and this entity among them) came in from the north country and took possession of the rule of this country, setting up the first dynasty. The entity was with that dynasty, also in the second dynasty of Araaraart, when those buildings were begun. The base of the sphinx was laid out in channels, and in the corner facing the Gizeh may be found the wording of how this was founded, giving the history of the first invading ruler and the ascension of Araaraart to that position.   (195-14)

This reading tells us that at the corner base of the Sphinx facing Gizeh (the Great Pyramid) is the wording of how the Sphinx was founded and the history of Arart and his son Araaraart. On this corner of the Sphinx is a small rectangle about ten feet high, which I call a "box." Located on the other side of the Sphinx near the right forepaw is another identical box.

One of these boxes of stone is by the corner facing the Great Pyramid, where records are located, according to Cayce, and the other box is by the right forepaw where the entrance to the Hall of Records is located. It may be a coincidence, but these boxes are located right where Cayce says there are underground chambers. Also significant is that no mention is made in any of the hieroglyphs concerning these boxes. Why? Perhaps they were to remain a secret until the time was ripe.

In the 1920s when the Sphinx was dug out of the sand, a statue of the Egyptian god of the underworld was found in pieces on top of the box by the right forepaw. Legend has it that a Pharaoh dismantled the box and discovered an underground passage leading from it. When his men went into the passage, they came out covered with painful sores. The Pharaoh had the box sealed and a statue of the god of the underworld placed on top of it. If this legend is true, the Pharaoh's men may have discovered the entrance to the Hall of Records, and then sealed it back up.

In 1982 S.R.I., Inc. (formerly Stanford Research Institute), did acoustical soundings underneath the right front paw of the Sphinx, and what they found is very interesting. Under the entire length of the right paw, they got a good clear signal, indicating there are no underground passages there. But directly under the right front paw box, the signal was dead in three places, as though some kind of opening or empty space were blocking the signal. These dead spots may be the passageway that the Pharaoh's men found.

When Cayce was alive, he did a series of readings for a man he said would be one of the ones to rediscover the Hall of Records. During the building of the Great Pyramid this man lived in Egypt, and his name at that time was Hept-supht. According to Cayce, Hept-supht means "keep it shut." He was in charge of closing up the records and keeping them shut until the time was right. He asked Cayce the following question:

> *Q. Am I the one to receive directions as to where the sealed room is and how to find it?*
>
> **A. One of the two. Two with a guide. Hept-supht, El-ka[?], and Atlan. These will appear.**
>
> **(378-16)**

Since the man asking the question died in 1960, it is apparent that he will make the discovery during a more recent incarnation, one that probably began in the last few years. Two others will appear to join him, Atlan and El-ka by their Atlantean names. Hept-supht will find the records because he was the one that sealed them thousands of years ago during an elaborate ceremony.

> **And, as this was to be (Gizeh we are speaking of) the place for the initiates and their gaining by personal application, and by the journey or journeys through the various activities – as in the ceremonial actions of those that became initiates, it became very fitting (to those as in Ra, and those of Ra-Ta Ra) that there should be the crowning or placing of this symbol of the record, and of the initiates' place of activity, by one who represented both the old and the new; one representing then the Sons of the Law in Atlantis, Lemuria, Oz and Og. So, he that keeps the record, that keeps shut, or Hept-supht, was made or chosen as the one to seal that in the tomb.**
>
> **The ceremony was long; the clanging of the apex by the gavel that was used in the sounding of the placing. Hence there has arisen from this ceremony many of those things that may be seen in the present; as the call to prayer, the church bell in the present, may be termed a descendant; the**

sounding of the trumpet as the call to arms, or that as revelry; the sound as of those that make for mourning, in the putting away of the body; the sounding as of ringing in the new year, the sounding as of the coming of the bridegroom; all have their inception from the sound that was made that kept the earth's record of the earth's building, as to that from the change. The old record in Gizeh is from that as recorded from the journey to Pyrenees; and to 1998 from the death of the Son of Man (as a man).   (378-14)

The following readings tell us when the records will be found:

As for the physical records – it will be necessary to wait until the full time has come for the breaking up of much that has been in the nature of selfish motives in the world. For, remember, these records were made from the angle of WORLD movements. So must thy activities be in the present of the universal approach, but as applied to the individual.   (2329-3)

For, as must be known to all God IS! And the soul that becomes more and more aware of His, God's use of man, that all may know of His Presence, is becoming then in at-onement; as self was in the experience, and preserved that record for the future entering souls, that will be physically known when time has set its mark.   (378-16)

This may not be entered without an understanding, for those that were left as guards may NOT be passed until after a period of their regeneration in the Mount, or the fifth root race begins.   (5748-6)

The records will not be found until there is the "breaking up of . . . selfish motives in the world," and "time has set its mark." Clearly, the selfish motives of the world will not be broken up until 1998, and so the opening of the Hall of Records will probably coincide with the Second Coming. Humanity could not handle the technological advances contained in the records without a spiritual understanding.

Cayce links the discovery of the records with the beginning of the "fifth root race," and according to the writings of Madam Blavatsky, the fifth root race, or the change of humanity to a more spiritual self, will not begin until Jesus returns. So this is more evidence that the Hall of Records will not be opened until 1998.

Jesus said, "I will bring all things to thine remembrance." This was not only a reference to the remembrance of past lives, but to the revelation of our whole history with the Second Coming. There will be no more debate between creationist and evolutionist. The true story of our creation and destiny will be known to *all*.

THE FIFTH ROOT RACE

While discussing how the Hall of Records might be found, Edgar Cayce gave the following information:

This may not be entered without an understanding, for those that were left as guards may NOT be passed until after a period of their regeneration in the Mount, or the fifth root race begins.

(5748-6)

Cayce tells us that the Hall of Records may not be entered until "the fifth root race begins." The question of course is, "What is a fifth root race?"

A root race is not a race like we normally think of in terms of black, white, yellow, brown, or red. The term "root race" refers to the human race or, as the scientists refer to it, *Homo sapiens*.

The idea of root races is well established in mystical tradition. The nineteenth-century mystic, Madam Blavatsky, referred to seven or more root races as preceding *Homo sapiens*. Cayce tells us that there were four previous root races, but as is often the case with the Cayce readings, no one asked Mr. Cayce what those four root races were. However, from my twenty years of study of the Cayce readings, I believe the four root races were spirit, thought form, projection into matter, and, finally, Adamic human, or *Homo sapiens*.

The Cayce readings tell us that there is going to be a new physical type of human being, which will begin around the time that the Hall of Records is opened in Egypt. Cayce tells us that the Hall of Records contains records that lead up to 1998, so I believe that this new root race will begin in 1998.

In order to get a better understanding of what all this means, I think it would be valuable for us to look back at Cayce's story of the history of humankind.

Cayce tells us that humans did not evolve from the apes. Cayce says that the souls were originally in the Spirit, and that there was a "rebellion in the celestial," and the souls began to project themselves into matter and became separated from God. He says that they could project themselves at will into matter, be it trees, rocks, animals, whatever. He says the souls "became the things that the minerals were."

Gradually, they took on a form that was denser than spirit, and Cayce called this form the "thought form." This makes sense since a mental form is more concentrated than pure Spirit. These thought forms had the ability to take shape in thought, "much in the way and manner as the amoeba would in the waters of a stagnant bay, or lake, in the present" (364-3).

These thought forms projected into matter, and their bodies hardened such that they became trapped in matter. Some souls became so trapped that they were little more than automatons, and Cayce called theses creatures the "things." They were bruteous creatures, and they took on many different forms such as giants and dwarfs. Genesis

6:4 tells us that "there were giants in the earth in those days. . ."

Interestingly enough, this aspect of Cayce's creation story is confirmed by anthropologists. Fossils have been discovered of giant humanoids such as Gigantopithecus, a human ancestor that stood over eight feet tall and weighed 400 to 500 pounds. In addition fossils of dwarflike human ancestors such as Australopithecus have also been discovered. These discoveries show us that there was indeed a great variety of forms in early human history.

After the souls became trapped in matter, other souls came into the earth to help – not by their own will, but by the will of God. Cayce called these souls, "the Sons of God." The Sons of God were androgynous, with both sexes being contained in one body.

> **In the beginning, as was outlined, there was presented that that became as the Sons of God, in that male and female were as one, with those abilities for those changes as were able or capable of being brought about.** **(364-7)**

The Sons of God had tremendous occult powers, but they, too, became entangled in matter and began to separate into male and female. Genesis 6:2 says that "the sons of God saw the daughters of men that they were fair; and they took them wives of all whom they chose." This is a poetic description of the separating of the Sons of God into male and female.

At this point there were many different forms on the earth. There were the things, the thought forms, the Sons of God, giants, dwarfs, etc. A group of the Sons of God led by one named Amilius realized that things were out of control, and one form needed to be created to accommodate all the different souls. So Amilius and the Sons of God created Adamic human or *Homo sapiens*. Cayce constantly quotes Job 38:7 in this regard:

"Where were you when I laid the foundations of the earth? When the morning stars sang together, and all the sons of God shouted for joy?"

Cayce tells us that the five races were projected into five different places simultaneously. The skin color of each race matching the soil where the projection took place. The white, the Caucasus; the black, Africa; the brown, India; the yellow, the Gobi; and the red, Atlantis.

Cayce's description of a simultaneous projection of *Homo sapiens* fits well with what anthropologists say happened to early humans. They tell us that about 33,000 B.C. *Homo sapiens* sprang forth and many of the older forms of humanoids became extinct. Scientists call this period the "Great Leap Forward." They call it this because during this period human culture became more sophisticated overnight. Sophisticated tools such as fishing hooks and bows and arrows appeared. Primitive art such as cave paintings became more sophisticated, as well. In Europe during this period the relatively primitive Neanderthal man became extinct, and *Homo sapiens*, or Adamic human, became the dominant form.

How was the Adamic human created? This was never fully explained in the Cayce readings, but one reading uses the term "introgression" (5748-6) to describe the process. The word "introgression" means gene splicing.

This is fascinating since scientists tell us that the difference between primitive human and modern human is a one percent change in our genetic material, DNA. Once again, the scientific information backs up Cayce's story of prehistory.

All of this leads us up to today, and the question of how the modern human is going to make this physical change to the fifth root race.

The only way that humans can change physically is by a change in their genetic code, DNA. But how does one's genetic code change? I see three distinct possibilities as agents of this change.

The first possibility is that we will change our own genetic code scientifically. Scientists are already doing this through gene splicing. They have learned how to change our genetic code by taking out DNA from our genes and replacing it with different DNA. In this way they have learned how to cure certain types of genetic defects in children. If a child has a defective gene that prevents his or her body from performing its proper function, scientists can now replace that gene with a nondefective gene so that the body will perform normally.

Other amazing things have been done with animals and plants. Recombinant DNA research has created mice with human lungs that help scientists do medical research. They have also combined a goat and a sheep to create a creature they call a "geep." They are currently working on making tomatoes that ripen at the grocery store, and vegetables that stay ripe for very long periods of time without refrigeration.

A project is under way to map all the human genes and their functions. This opens up tremendous possibilities. Besides curing genetic diseases, scientists might discover genes for mathematical ability, musical ability, and athletic ability that they could genetically engineer into a person's body. There is also the possibility that genes will be discovered that will slow or reverse the aging process. Scientists have already been able to double the life span of certain animals through genetic engineering. They may be able to create a completely new type of human being – the fifth root race that Cayce talks about.

The second possible cause for a change in our genetic code involves Cayce's predicted earth changes for the end of this decade. Cayce predicts that in 1998 there will be a pole shift on the earth. This may be a shift in the earth's magnetic poles, which scientists tell us periodically reverse themselves. When the earth's magnetic poles reverse themselves, the earth's magnetic field drops to zero. The earth's magnetic field is the only thing that protects the earth from exposure to cosmic radiation. By studying past magnetic field reversals and fossil records, scientists have discovered that when the earth's magnetic field reverses, old forms of life die and new ones appear. Scientists theorize that this is because exposure to cosmic radiation can cause genetic mutations. So the predicted pole shift could expose people on the earth to cosmic radiation that could cause them to change genetically into another form.

Interestingly enough, scientists believe we are currently in the beginning of a magnetic field reversal. They have discovered that the strength of the earth's magnetic field has dropped by 15% in the last 300 years. At that rate the earth's magnetic field will reverse itself in another 1,500 years. Even more worrisome is the fact that some scientists theorize that the rate of decrease could accelerate, and the field could reverse much faster.

The third possible agent of change that could create a fifth root race is what I call the supernatural event. This involves the direct intervention of angelic forces on the earth. This seems to be the way that *Homo sapiens*, or the fourth root race, was created. Cayce says that the five races were projected to five places simultaneously by the Sons of God. The same kind of thing could occur again. There is evidence for this in the Cayce readings and the Bible:

1 Corinthians 15:51-52

Behold, I show you a mystery: We shall not all sleep, but we shall all be changed.

In a moment, in the twinkling of an eye, at the last trumpet; for the trumpet shall sound, and the dead shall be raised incorruptible, and we shall be changed.

These verses from Corinthians tell us that "we shall all be changed." Could this refer to the change of the human body to the fifth root race? I think it could. This passage also gives us the time frame for this event. It says that this will occur "at the last trumpet." In Matthew 24 Jesus tells us that the last trumpet will be sounded with His return to earth. Cayce says that Jesus will return in 1998. So I believe the fifth root race will begin in 1998.

Cayce himself was asked about the meaning of this section of 1 Corinthians. This is what he said:

> *Q. Please explain 1 Cor. 15:51. Is the reference here to the body? "Behold, I show you a mystery. We shall not all sleep, but we shall all be changed."*
>
> **A. Referring to the body; though the individual here speaking (Paul) LOOKED for this to happen in his own day, see?** (262-87)

Cayce tells us that this passage of Corinthians refers to the body. Then he goes on to say that Paul expected this change to happen in his own day, thus implying that this change will happen in the future. That is what I think will happen.

There are other passages in the Bible that refer to this event:

Thessalonians 4:16-17

For the Lord himself shall descend from heaven with a shout, with the voice of the archangel, and with the trumpet of God; and the dead in Christ shall rise first.

Then we who are alive and remain shall be caught up together with them in the clouds, to meet the Lord in the air; and so shall we ever be with the Lord.

Once again, we see that the trumpet is mentioned in the description of the return of Jesus. This is the "Lord himself shalt descend from heaven with a shout" verse. In another parallel with 1 Corinthians, 1 Thessalonians says that the "dead in Christ shall rise first." Finally, there is a reference to those "who are alive" being "caught up together with them in the clouds." So something will happen to those people who are alive. I believe this "something" will be the creation of the new root race Cayce talks about.

Cayce echoes 1 Thessalonians in the following reading:

> **He will not tarry, for having overcome He shall appear even AS the Lord AND Master. Not as one born, but as one that returneth to His own, for He will walk and talk with men of every clime, and those that are faithful and just in their reckoning shall be caught up with Him to rule and to do JUDGMENT for a thousand years!   (364-7)**

Cayce discusses the return of Jesus as one who "will walk and talk with men of every clime." He then goes on to quote 1 Thessalonians when he says that those who are "faithful and just in their reckoning shall be caught up with Him to rule and to do judgment for a thousand years." "Caught up" definitely implies some sort of change for the people involved.

Other readings also seem to imply this change.

> **As to times, as to seasons, as to places, ALONE is it given to those who have named the name – and who bear the mark of those of His calling and His election in their bodies. To them it shall be given.**
> **(3976-15)**

This reading talks about those "who bear the mark of those of His calling and His election in their bodies." Now that's a curious phrase. Not those who bear the mark of His calling in their hearts or minds or souls but in their bodies. This could be a reference to the change of our bodies to a new root race.

The following reading also seems to imply a change in us with Jesus' return.

> **So, as He [Jesus] gave, "I leave thee, but I will come again and receive as many as ye have quickened through the manifesting in thy life the will of the Father in the earth."** (262-58)

Jesus will come again and receive those who have "quickened."

All of these quotes from the Bible and the Cayce readings refer to some kind of action. We shall all be "changed," we shall be "caught up," we shall be "quickened." I believe all these references refer to the creation of the fifth root race. What will this new root race be like? We don't really know. We do know that it will be more evolved than we are at the present. Perhaps we will be like the Sons of God with androgynous bodies and occult powers. We may evolve into something totally different than we have ever seen before. We can only speculate, but if Mr. Cayce is correct, we only have a short time to wait to find out what this new root race will be like.

NOSTRADAMUS AND THE HOPI INDIANS

Nostradamus

Michel de Nostradamus is the most famous prophet in French history. He lived during the sixteenth century, and his abilities as a prognosticator earned him fame far and wide. He made many predictions of the future, including some applicable to our time, and it is for this reason he is of interest to us.

Nostradamus was born in St. Remy de Provence, France, on December 14, 1503. His family was of Jewish descent but converted to Catholicism when Michael was very young. His intellect soon became apparent to everyone, and so in 1522 at the age of nineteen, he was sent to France's most prestigious college of medicine at Montpellier.

During his stay at school, the Black Plague struck southern France, and Nostradamus was pressed into service to fight it. He showed great courage during this time, healing the sick when most doctors had moved on to avoid catching the plague themselves. He traveled for several years, then returned to Montpellier to complete his doctorate.

After getting married and settling down to what would seem to have been an idyllic life in Agen, tragedy struck Nostradamus. His wife and children died of plague, ruining his reputation as a healer. Then the church began to investigate him in connection with the Inquisition, because he had made some careless remarks about a statue of the Virgin Mary that was being erected in town. He was also suspicious to authorities because he refused to bleed his patients, a common practice at that time. Nostradamus was forced to travel to avoid persecution, and it was during these travels that he first began to make predictions about the affairs of humankind.

Legend has it that during his travels through Italy he passed a monk on the street. Nostradamus suddenly knelt down and called the monk "your holiness." The monk must certainly have been startled since he was only a swineherd at the time, not a member of the church hierarchy. Years later in 1585, the monk, Felice Peretti, became Pope Sixtus V. Nostradamus's amazing powers had allowed him to see the future perfectly.

Presumably because of such flashes of insight, Nostradamus began to write *The Prognostications*, his first book of prophecy, which he published in 1554. Encouraged by the success of his first book, he produced his now famous book, *The Prophecies*. This book was an even bigger hit than his first, and Nostradamus was called to Paris for an audience with the queen, Catherine de Medici. He spoke with the queen for two hours and stayed on in Paris for several weeks, drawing up horoscopes and offering prophetic advice. Soon, the justices of Paris began to investigate him for his magic practices, and he returned home to Salon. It is there he spent the rest of his days until he died in 1566.

A revival of interest in Nostradamus began during World War II when Frau Goebbels showed her husband, the German propaganda minister, some of Nostradamus's prophecies that appeared to apply to Adolph Hitler. Dr. Goebbels was intrigued and decided to use them as evidence of Hitler's divine destiny to be ruler of Europe. Goebbels hired an astrologer named Krafft to produce propaganda based on the writings of Nostradamus. The British, fearful that the German ploy would have a negative psychological effect on occupied Europe, developed retaliatory leaflets and had them dropped by airplane over the occupied countries. It is doubtful that this propaganda war had any effect on the real one, but the prophecies were convincing enough to cause action on both sides. From them we can see why:

11-24

Beasts wild with hunger will cross the rivers, the greater part of the battlefield will be against Hister. He will drag the leader in a cage of iron, when the child of Germany observes no law.

Nostradamus purposely wrote his prophecy in vague style to avoid persecution by the church. Thus the name Hister could easily be an anagram for Hitler. This quatrain (as Nostradamus's prophecies were called) refers to all against Hister on the battlefield, as was the case with Hitler in World War II. Given the atrocities committed by the Nazis during this time, the "child of Germany observes no law" fits as well. We can see very easily how this particular quatrain applied to Hitler and the Nazis, giving credence to the prophetic abilities of Michel de Nostradamus.

With the rash of gloom and doom prophecies now appearing, it is not surprising that the writings of Nostradamus have experienced a revival. Most of his prophecies involve death, war, and famine written as only one who had seen the Black Plague could have written them. Many of the quatrains are senseless and confusing, but some like the Hister quatrains are accurate, making it impossible to dismiss Nostradamus's abilities entirely.

The following quatrain predicts a tribulation before the end of this century:

> **1146**
> **After great misery for mankind**
> **an even greater approaches**
> **when the great cycle of the**
> **centuries is renewed. It will**
> **rain blood, milk, famine, war and disease:**
> **In the sky will be seen a fire, dragging**
> **a trail of sparks.**

The end of the cycle of the centuries is the year 2000, and this fits perfectly into the pattern of prophecies we have seen predicting a tribulation at the end of this century. War and famine are mentioned as expected. In addition, a fire dragging a trail of sparks could be the appearance of a comet as a celestial harbinger of things to come. Another possibility is that this is Nostradamus's description of a missile, something he would not have seen in the sixteenth century and therefore would have no way of describing. The following quatrain describes the great famine:

> **1-67**
> **The great famine which I sense approaching will often turn (in various areas) then become worldwide. It will be so vast and long lasting that (they) will grab roots from the trees and children from the breast.**

This is a frightening description by which we can see

the gloomy tone of the quatrains. Clearly Nostradamus felt we were in for devastating famine, so much so that people will eat the roots from the trees.

A number of the quatrains mentions the Anti-Christ, and the following hints at an Anti-Christ empire:

111-97

A new law will occupy a new
land around Syria, Judea, and Palestine.
The great barbarian Empire will crumble before
the century of the sun is finished.

This quatrain has been interpreted as describing the birth of the state of Israel. The "century of the sun" is the twentieth century, and a "great barbarian Empire" will crumble before this century is through. From this quatrain and others describing an Anti-Christ from the East, people have predicted an Arab and also a Chinese Anti-Christ. The following quatrain is important in that connection:

X-72

In the year 1999, and seven
months, from the sky will come the great
King of Terror. He
will bring to life the great
king of the Mongols. Before and after War
reigns happily.

The date here, 1999, is very close to Cayce's date of 1998, a fascinating coincidence to say the least. During this period a great "King of Terror" will bring back to life the great "king of the Mongols," and war will reign. This dregs up visions of the army of 200 million in Revelation. Nostradamus may have been describing those verses from The Revelation, as he must surely have been a student of the Bible. This, however, is pure speculation. In any case this quatrain comes close to the picture of the future we have gleaned from other sources.

To sum up, Nostradamus predicts war and famine toward the turn of the century along with an Asian Anti-Christ. His prophecies predict a comet will appear in association with these events. Fortunately, we know that if Nostradamus was right about his gloom, doom, death, and destruction prophecies, the period following will be the joyous millennium humankind has looked forward to for so long.

The Hopi Indians

The Hopi Indians of the American Southwest have a long, deep, and spiritual history. The Hopi live on the Black Mesa of northeastern Arizona, an area of land which rises thousands of feet above the surrounding plain. They live a simple way of life, farming and maintaining the rhythm of life that has been theirs for thousands of years. They have never been to war with the white man, preferring to remain a separate entity. This nature is reflected in their name, Hopi, which means "peaceful people."

The Hopi's story of creation is almost identical to our own. In the beginning the Taiowa (the Infinite) created the Sotuknang (the Finite); and God (the Infinite) created the heavens and the earth (the Finite). Taiowa ordered Sotuknang to create the twins, Poquanghoya and Palongawhoya. Poquanghoya and Palongawhoya were sent to the North and South Poles to keep the earth turning. This legend of a positive and negative force corresponds with what scientists tell us was the first element, hydrogen, which is made of one positive particle, the proton, and one negative particle, the electron.

The Hopi have a history of several worlds preceding the present one, each destroyed by calamity. These worlds were destroyed by the same things that many other sources tell us were the methods of destruction in our own history: fire, ice, and flood. According to the Hopi, during the first world, life was in harmony with the infinite. People gradually fell out of harmony with the infinite, however, and according to the *Bear Tribe's Self-Reliance Book* (which recounts Hopi history) we "lost the use of the vibratory center on the top of the head (kopave), and the soft spot that was the doorway between the body and the spirit hardened." This fits with what we know about the pituitary gland, the psychic center in the brain where we can attune to the infinite. The Hopi thus recorded what we know as the Fall from Grace in their legends.

The Hopi record that God destroyed the First World by fire.

"Taiowa decided that would never do, and so he ordered Sotuknang to destroy the world, but to save a few people from destruction. He led them into the center of the world, where they were received by the Ant People. The Ant People fed them so well that they, themselves, began to grow thin. (It is said that this is the reason why today the Ant People have such thin waists.) As the people stayed underground, the volcanoes on the surface of the First World erupted, and the whole world caught fire. After the fires subsided, the people came up from their shelter and began to move to the Second World that had been prepared for them."

The Second World was destroyed by ice.

"Here, again, the people lived until they forgot their origin and grew cold and hard to the ways of the Good Life. And so, once again, Sotuknang was ordered to destroy the world. This time he ordered the Twins, Poquanghoya and Palongawhoya, to leave their stations at the North and South Poles and let the world be destroyed. They did this, after the people had again hidden with the Ant People underground. After the Twins left their stations, the world's stability was removed, and so it flipped end over end and everything on it was destroyed by ice."

This legend of a pole shift and an ice age agrees with what we have learned about the last pole shift, which occurred approximately 45,000-48,000 B.C.

The world before the present one was, according to the Hopi, destroyed by the flood. This corresponds to all the legends and history of the so-called "Great Flood." The story of Noah and his ark is the one most of us are familiar with in this regard. Taiowa destroyed the last world by sending high waves over the continents. This fits with the description in the Cayce readings of the destruction of Atlantis, an event that preceded the present era. Of course, the sinking of the continent of Atlantis is recorded in other sources as well, including Plato. All this brings us to the Fourth World of today.

What interests us about the Hopi's view of the Fourth World is its future. The Hopi tradition includes prophecies just like the white man's. The culmination of these prophecies will be Purification Day, when evil will be eliminated and peace will rule the land. Several events were predicted by the Hopi leading up to Purification Day. Wagons linked together and pulled by something other than a horse was one of the first signs predicted. This was fulfilled by the white man's railroad. Cobwebs in the air, roads in the sky, and lines across the land were also predicted. Airline routes and highways fulfilled these prophecies.

A "gourd full of ashes" would be invented, according to the Hopi, which would cause destruction, boiling rivers, and burning land. The Hopi believe the explosion of the Hiroshima atomic bomb fulfilled this prophecy.

One of the last signs will be when the white man puts his "house in the sky." After that, great changes will be in store for the people of the earth. Our meddling with the forces of nature will cause the earth and its people to be out of balance, creating great destruction. The Hopi believe that the United States space station Skylab was the "house in the sky" of their prophecy. Skylab was launched in the mid-1970s.

The religious leaders of the Hopi tribe, the spiritual elders, decided in 1948 that the prophecies were beginning to come true and they should act. First, they decided to reveal to the world the prophecies of their people. One part of these prophecies foretold of a great "house of mica" standing on the eastern shore of America that would be a place where the leaders of the world would assemble. Mica is very similar to glass, and the Hopi interpreted this to be a reference to the United Nations building in New York City. The Hopi were to go to the house of mica three times, and if they were rejected, then they were to return to their home and await the Day of Purification.

Twice the Hopi went to the General Assembly, in 1948 and 1973, and both times they were not allowed to speak. In 1976 after two attempts, the Hopi were allowed to speak at a U.N.-sponsored Habitat Conference in Vancouver. Their speaker was Thomas Banyacya, their religious leader. Part of his speech follows:

> "The message today is our third and perhaps final attempt to inform the world of the present status of man's existence on our Earth Mother. We are not asking the United Nations for help in any material way. We are, according to Hopi prophecy, simply trying to inform the world of what is going to happen if the destruction of the earth and its original peoples continues as is known by our religious Hopi elders. We do not come before the United Nations in order to join it. We come to fulfill Hopi sacred mission and ancient prophecy in

order to find one, two, or three nations who should now recognize their sacred duty to stop the destruction of the First People's land and life throughout the Western Hemisphere. We, Hopi, know that there are one, two, or three nations here in the United Nations that could listen to our message and understand it so that they can fulfill their mission, and whatever results from your failure to fulfill your sacred responsibilities to stop all of this destruction, genocide, harassment, imprisonment, oppression, and lack of respect for Native Brothers will be of your own doing because we, the First Peoples of the Western Hemisphere, have carried out our sacred duty by bringing this spiritual message of warnings and hope for the future to your attention."

One of the keys to the Hopi prophecy is their interpretation of a petroglyph that is carved on rock in the middle of the Hopi Black Mesa.

The knowledge of world events has been handed down in secret religious societies of the Hopi. The leaders throughout each generation have especially watched for a series of three world-shaking events, each accompanied by a particular symbol. These symbols – the swastika, the sun, and the color red – are inscribed upon a rock and on the sacred gourd rattle used in Hopi ceremonies. From the sacred teachings the Hopi knew that out of the violence and destruction of each world-shaking and purifying experience, the strongest elements would emerge with a greater force to produce the next event. (World War II, championed by Germany and its swastika, merged later with Japan, "land of the rising sun.") When these symbols appeared on the international scene, it was very clear to the Hopi that a major and final phase of world prophecy was being fulfilled, and they then released for humanity (in 1948) many of the secret teachings in order to help offset the third and final "great purification" which on the petroglyph is portrayed by a red hat and cloak. According to the Hopi elders, "The red hat and cloak people will have a huge population." They will invade this land in a single day "like a swarm of locusts" and the sky will be darkened with them as they come. This prophecy is similar to the biblical Revelation which speaks of the great red dragon which threatens nations and the invasion by "the Kings of the East" and 200 million horsemen.

As we can see, the Hopi prophecy fits Revelation's description of an invasion by a massive army, possibly the Chinese. The red hat and cloak fit this imagery since the symbol of the Chinese is the communist red flag. In addition, the Chinese army has a red insignia on their uniforms. The Hopi prediction that the sky will be darkened during this time agrees with the Bible's prediction. All of this is associated with a Day of Purification paralleling the "Judgment Day" of the Bible.

The Purification Day will bring the return of the True White Brother, according to the Hopi. The True White Brother will be one of the people who will cause the Purification Day to occur. The story of this True White Brother is as follows:

After the destruction of the Third World by Flood, the Great Spirit created a set of stone tablets which contained all the teachings, prophecies, and warnings necessary for the safety of the Fourth World. These stone tablets were given to the Hopi chief who led the tribe into their present home, after the destruction of the Third World. The stone tablets were to provide the information for maintaining the harmony and balance of the new world.

The chief left the tablets to his two sons when he died, dividing them between the two. The older brother took one of the tablets east. After reaching the East, he was to return and look for his younger brother, and together they were to bring about the Purification Day, so that evil could be eliminated from the earth, and harmony return. The brothers would know each other because they would have matching stone tablets. The younger brother would recognize his older brother because he would have a lighter complexion, a true white brother (thus the name), and would be wearing a red cap or a red cloak. This is the myth the Hopi have retained of the True White Brother.

Of course, our point of view is that the True White Brother is Jesus and that the Purification Day is what we call Judgment Day. All of this once again fits the Bible's view. Even more interesting is the reference to stone tablets which detail a plan for harmony and balance. Could this be the Hall of Records in Egypt? They contain teachings and prophecies just like the ones described in the Hopi prophecy. The Egyptian records were made and put away just after the destruction of the Third World, another parallel to the prophecies of the Hopi. The legend of the stone tablets may be a historical account of the Hall of Records passed down through generations and generations of Hopi.

The *Mexico Mystique* by Frank Waters tells us more about the Day of Purification.

"As the Day of Purification approaches, the True White Brother will come. He will bring with him sacred stone tablets to match those given the Hopis long ago. With him will come two helpers. One will carry the swastika, male symbol of purity, and a cross, female symbol of purity. The second helper will carry the symbol of the sun. These two will shake the earth. There will be a massive explosion, perhaps a volcanic eruption that will be felt throughout North and South America.

"If these three fulfill their mission, finding a few Hopis who steadfastly adhere to their ancient teachings, they will lay out a new life plan. The earth will become new as it was in the beginning. The people saved will share everything in common, speak one tongue, and adopt the religion of the Great Spirit, Massau. But if the three sacred beings fail in their mission, and all people still remain corrupt, the Great Spirit will send 'One' from the West. He will be many, many people and unmerciful. He will destroy the earth, only the ants being left to inhabit it."

This passage parallels the earth changes predicted in the Bible. The concept of the millennium is described by the Hopi as the world adopting the religion of the Great Spirit and sharing resources in common.

Tom Tarbet in an article entitled "The Essence of Hopi Prophecy" from the *East West Journal* (October 1977) tells us more:

"The final stage, called the 'great day of purification,' has also been described as a 'mystery egg,' in which the forces of the swastika and the sun, plus a third force, symbolized by the color red, culminate in either total rebirth or total annihilation – we don't yet know which, but the choice is ours. War and natural catastrophe may be involved, the degree of violence determined by the degree of inequity among the peoples of the world, and the amount of imbalance in nature. In this crisis, rich and poor will be forced to struggle as equals to survive.

"That it will be very violent is now almost taken for granted among traditional Hopi, but humans may still lessen the violence by correcting their treatment of nature and fellow humans. Ancient spiritually based communities, such as the Hopi, must especially be preserved and not forced to abandon their wise way of life and the natural resources they have vowed to protect."

The Hopi believe, as do many others, that the degree of violence associated with the coming changes is dependent upon how well humanity is in harmony with the earth and the Great Spirit, God. If there is equality among the nations and people of the world, then the changes will be less severe. If we upset the "balance of nature" by our actions with respect to the earth, then the earth will react violently.

The Hopi prophecies agree with the other prophecies we have looked at in several different categories.

1. There will be a Purification Day when wickedness will be destroyed (Judgment Day).

2. There will be an invasion by a country with a large population (army of 200 million in Revelation).

3. The sky will be darkened.

4. Tablets will be revealed containing ancient teachings (Egyptian Hall of Records).

5. A True White Brother will return on Purification Day (Jesus' return).

6. Earth changes will accompany this Day of Purification.

7. The world will live in harmony and adopt one religion (the millennium).

All in all, the Hopi prophecies parallel the Bible remarkably, hitting almost all the same key points. It shows that religions of different cultures can arrive at the same conclusions from different paths. These prophecies also make the Bible seem even more amazing, since most of its prophets made these same predictions 2,000 or more years ago.

The Hopi through time have shown themselves to be a spiritual people. The accuracy of their prophecies confirms this. It is hoped that the world will listen to their warning and prepare in harmony before the Day of Purification comes.

FIVE GREAT THINGS THAT WILL HAPPEN IN 1998

The New Age

There is very little in the prophecies to tell us what the New Age will be like. So I went back and looked at the Edgar Cayce readings on Atlantis to get some kind of glimpse at what the future may be like.

Cayce tells us that the continent of Atlantis existed at a very high spiritual and technological level for thousands of years. He says that Atlantis was ruled by a man named Amilius who, according to Cayce, was a previous incarnation of Jesus.

The Atlanteans had a crystal power source and could beam this power from place to place. In addition Cayce says they had the ability to transpose matter from one end of the universe to the next, just like they beam things from place to place on *Star Trek*.

The Atlanteans also had a spiritual understanding that included the use of occult powers such as telepathy, telekinesis, etc. Cayce says that among the Atlanteans such powers were commonplace.

One of the most interesting descriptions of Atlantis in the Cayce readings involves a crystal room. Apparently, the initiates would enter this room with an enormous crystal in the center and go into an altered state of consciousness, that is, go out of the body. Then through this crystal they could communicate with what Cayce called "angelic forces." These are the kinds of things we have to look forward to in the future!

Five Great Things That Will Happen in 1998

In the 1990s everything needs to be reduced to the level of a sound bite. Here is my version of this book's sound bite. I call it Five Great Things That Will Happen in 1998.

1. The Opening of the Hall of Records

Cayce tells us that a repository of ancient knowledge, which he refers to as the Hall of Records, will be opened in 1998. He says that these records are in three places: underwater off the coast of Bimini, in the Yucatan in Central America, and by the Sphinx in Egypt.

2. A New Type of Human Body

The Cayce readings say that there will be a new type of human body beginning in 1998. He calls this new body the fifth root race. This is not a race like we normally think of race as in black, white, yellow, brown, and red, but a new human race with a new type of physical body.

3. A Public Answer to the UFO Mystery

I believe that part of the opening of awareness in 1998 will be a public answer to the UFO mystery. This does not come from any prophetic sources, but from my own personal intuitive feeling.

4. A Thousand Years of Peace on the Earth

Both the Bible and Edgar Cayce tell us that there will be a thousand years of peace on the earth. No more war, bloodshed, or oppression will happen anywhere in the world. It will be the greatest time in human history. And it will begin in 1998.

5. The Second Coming of Jesus

The return of Jesus to Earth.

Conclusion

As time goes by, I believe we need to give more and more thought about our own attitude toward the Second Coming. The great tribulation and the changes in the earth are merely the birth pains of a new age, something which is unpleasant but which must be experienced if this new world is to be born. We should not look on the changes with fear, even though it is hard not to sometimes. As Richard Bach wrote in his book *Illusions*, "What the caterpillar calls the end of the world, the master calls a butterfly." It all depends on your point of view when you look at it.

The Second Coming itself will, I am sure, be totally different than we think it will be. It will be more dynamic and beautiful and will affect more people than we can imagine. The entire world will undergo a tremendous transformation, a revolutionary change on all levels. People will feel the urgency of this change as we approach the end of this century. They will feel a sense of Jesus' presence, both in a physical sense with His appearance and in the individual sense within their own hearts. For it is within our hearts that we meet the Christ.

When Jesus appears, He will be loving and forgiving. He will embody all the positive characteristics a human being can have. He will be as wonderful as we expect Him to be, and more. . . God's love flowing through one man.

His mere physical appearance is not the extent of the change, however, for He stood in people's presence 2,000 years ago, and it did not change their hard hearts. Thus, the change must be within us, and as such we all have a part in the Second Coming. This is a great opportunity for all of us, for we can be a part of the most joyous change in the history of humankind. No one will be kept from participating if he or she wants to.

We need to prepare ourselves mentally and spiritually for this new day, first through the desire to be a part of it and then through actions to make it come about in a more positive fashion. If in our day-to-day living we reflect God's love, we will be contributing positively to the atmosphere of expectancy. If we can be a little kinder, a little more forgiving, we will be contributing to the change. This is surely what is needed in the world today.

In the way of physical preparations, these need to be made, but this has been overemphasized by many people. It is said that we should head for the countryside, build fortresses, store food, and prepare for the end. The term "survivalists" has been coined by the press to describe people who preach this type of preparation. Even though storing food may be a good idea, in general the "survivalist" attitude isn't the best attitude to take. John White, author of *Pole Shift*, tells a story about a group of survivalists in Oregon. They bought land in the country, built underground bunkers, stored food, brought in their yogurt makers and Browning automatic rifles to prepare themselves for the disintegration of society at the end of the age. A year after the group formed, the leader died of a heart attack. The doctors said it was stress related! Obviously, he took the wrong attitude toward the coming changes, seeing them as confrontational. Our mental and spiritual preparation is more important than the physical. No amount of physical preparation is going to save you if you are not ready spiritually.

The millennium itself is something to be looked forward to with great joy. Political, economic, and social institutions will be set up on a much more equitable basis than they are today. No wars, strife, civil disorder, oppression, or denial of people's rights will be tolerated. Jesus will rule the nations with a "rod of iron." No more will the nations of the world waste $800 billion a year on weapons of destruction as they do today. Those resources will go to the improvement of life for every individual soul on the earth.

A new brand of science will emerge based on the understanding of the One Force in the universe. This science will extend life expectancy far beyond what it is today. People will live a long, long time, as we are told they did in biblical times. Some may live as long as Methuselah who, according to the Bible, lived to be over 900 years old.

The purpose of the millennium will not be just to snatch a few souls up to heaven, leaving the rest behind. Rather, the purpose of the millennium is to continue the work of saving souls from separation from God. The greatest sin is to be separated from God or to be unaware of His presence, and a soul can only will this on itself. For as has been said, "God has not willed that any soul should perish but has prepared for each a way of escape." An all-knowing, all-loving God would not want for any to perish, not *one*. So during the millennium and after, the work of soul attunement will go on. No souls will be lost unless they will it.

All that is necessary for us to be a part of the millennium is a desire to be there and the willingness to align our wills with God's will. I hope that everyone who reads this will experience the great joy that lies ahead.

Revelation 7:14-17

. . .These are they who came out of the great

tribulation, and have washed their robes, and made them white in the blood of the Lamb.

Therefore are they before the throne of God and serve him day and night in his temple; and he that sits on the throne shall dwell among them.

They shall hunger no more, neither thirst any more; neither shall the sun light on them, nor any heat.

For the Lamb who is in the midst of the throne shall feed them and shall lead them to living fountains of waters;

And God shall wipe away all tears from their eyes.

A.R.E. PRESS

The A.R.E. Press publishes quality books, videos, and audiotapes meant to improve the quality of our readers' lives—personally, professionally, and spiritually. We hope our products support your endeavors to realize your career potential, to enhance your relationships, to improve your health, and to encourage you to make the changes necessary to live a loving, joyful, and fulfilling life.

For more information or to receive a free catalog, call

        1-800-723-1112

Or write

        A.R.E. Press
        P.O. Box 656
        Virginia Beach, VA 23451-0656